4-28-75

FROM SERFDOM TO SOCIALISM
LABOUR AND THE EMPIRE
THE SOCIALIST'S BUDGET

FROM SERFDOM TO SOCIALISM
James Keir Hardie

LABOUR AND THE EMPIRE
James Ramsay MacDonald

THE SOCIALIST'S BUDGET
Philip Snowden

Edited with an introduction by
ROBERT E. DOWSE
Department of Politics,
University of Exeter

Rutherford . Madison . Teaneck
Fairleigh Dickinson University Press

First American edition published 1974 by:
ASSOCIATED UNIVERSITY PRESSES, INC.
Cranbury, New Jersey 08512

'From Serfdom to Socialism', 'Labour and the Empire' and
'The Socialist's Budget' first published in 1907 by George
Allen, London
'From Serfdom to Socialism', 'Labour and the Empire' and
'The Socialist's Budget' © George Allen & Unwin Ltd.,
London 1907, 1974

Introduction © Robert E. Dowse 1974

Library of Congress Catalogue Number 74-496
ISBN 0-8386-1540-6

Typesetting by Campbell Graphics Ltd., Newcastle upon Tyne
Printed in England by Redwood Press Limited, Trowbridge
Bound by Cedric Chivers Limited, Portway, Bath

Contents

Introduction by Robert E. Dowse   page vii

James Keir Hardie
FROM SERFDOM TO SOCIALISM

James Ramsay MacDonald
LABOUR AND THE EMPIRE

Philip Snowden
THE SOCIALIST'S BUDGET

Introduction

The short monographs which constitute the bulk of this volume were first published as separate volumes in 1906/7.* The series was intended by the publisher to meet an imputed public demand for hard information about the principles and policies of the Labour Party. Evidence for such a need may well have been inferred from the fact that fifty candidates fought the 1906 election on behalf of the Labour Representation Committee and that they obtained about 37% (300,000) of the votes cast in those constituencies. Certainly the success of the LRC in obtaining twenty-nine seats in that election would have confirmed the inference. In the popular imagination it is probable that the socialist was a political version of the wild man from Borneo: strange, foreign and a bit woolly. Socialists had curious ideas about sharing property, they wore odd clothes—which, perhaps, concealed bombs—and their morals left more than a little to be desired. In fine, the socialist was an anarchist and personally a bizarre creature, and insofar as his ideas were known at all they were misunderstood. *The Man Who Was Thursday* versus

---

*Together with the three reprinted here, three others made up the series: Ethel Snowden, *The Woman Socialist* (1907), Frederick W. Jowett, *The Socialist and the City* (1907), and Stewart D. Headlam, *The Socialist's Church* (1907). Collectively the six volumes were entitled *The Labour Ideal.*

The Secret of The League epitomised socialism for
the middle brow whilst *Vera* and *The Devils*
represented the socialist vision for the higher brow.

These three volumes illustrated socialist thinking
in Britain, or, rather, the thinking of the *parliamentary* section of British socialism. Intended as a
popular exposition of moderate socialism, not as a
contribution to factional polemic, the volumes, for
this reason alone, set out starkly and clearly the
strengths and weaknesses of the British parliamentary socialist tradition. In this introductory
essay I intend to examine the works from the
perspective of the 1920s, when it appeared that the
Labour Party had an opportunity to impress itself
on the major political institutions of this
country—rather than passively to receive their
impress—and yet failed to do so.

A standard account of the Labour Party's failure
to seize the opportunity presented by the electoral
and economic situation of the 1920s traces the
cause back to the ideology of the movement.
Writing of 1931 Ralph Miliband suggests that 'The
Labour movement *was* betrayed, but not because
the Labour Leaders were villains, or cowards. It
was betrayed because betrayal was the inherent
and inescapable consequence of their whole
philosophy of politics'.[1] Commenting on the
obvious failure of the second Labour Government
even to look as though it had any idea what to do
about the mounting economic crisis, John Paton
(one of the most intelligent ILP critics of the
Government), lamented that 'we believe the timid
policies of the Government do not spring from
their minority position, but from the adoption of

wrong views on policy which would be equally evident if they were a majority. At bottom, their weak policies are an expression of their belief in political gradualism'.[2] This view of the 1920s is crucially dependent upon two underlying assumptions. Firstly, that the ideas of the parliamentary leadership in fact *were* gradualist or reformist and, secondly, that the political paralysis which certainly did overtake the party was *caused* by the ideas they held.

The three essays here reprinted (together with the companion volumes) demonstrate beyond any reasonable doubt that their authors were not socialist theoreticians of even the second rank. Occasionally the word 'theory' creeps in, and in his introduction Ramsay MacDonald writes of 'political axioms' upon which Labour's imperial policy would be based; but this is a fustian rhetoric and does not underpin any policy suggestion in his contribution to the series—or yet his government's actual policies.[3] There is not a sign of a consistent and articulated ideology derived from any fundamental proposition about the nature of capitalist society which the authors share; indeed, they are often in quite radical disagreement with one another. In order to examine the idea that Labour failed because its ideology was weak it is necessary to isolate the various strands of ideas and assumptions detectable in the essays.

Firstly, and this is quite typical of the eclectic nature of Labour politics, one cannot but be struck by the assumption that socialism is really a culmination of all good things and an end product of historical development. History, so to say, stops with socialism. As Hardie puts it: 'Every popular movement of the past seven-hundred years has been a socialist movement at bottom'. (Hardie, p.84).* Socialism becomes simply an approval word used by good men to commend some of the past and to yearn for a better future. This is, of course, simply the Fabian argument concerning the inevitability of collectivism in a complex society taken back a few more hundred years. Closely akin to this way of looking at social development and again very typical of the essays is the sentiment so clearly expressed by Ethel Snowden: 'We have already travelled far along the road which leads to Socialism. Each day sees some fresh application or extended application of its principles'.[4] No human agency seems necessary to this process: 'It is coming; nothing can prevent that. It is the next inevitable step in ordered progress.'[5] Although it is not clear what the actual mechanism of in-evitability is, it appears that the process is a psycho-political one. Adult male suffrage is in stark contradiction to economic bondage, and the 'veritable Helot' as Hardie calls him, 'will use the political freedom which his father won for him to win industrial freedom for his children'. (Hardie, p.77). Realising the contradiction between economic bondage and political freedom the working man will insist that his economic life be brought into line with his political situation.[6]

Progress was inevitable and even opponents of socialism are driven to accept it since: 'In actual

---

*Unless otherwise noted, all quotations are from one or another volume of the series. All page references are to the original editions.

practice the individualist, so-called, accepts certain established services that are Socialistic in principle. He accepts them because they exist'.[7] Presumably the idea is that one morning Britain will wake up to find itself a socialist society with or without a Labour Government, although the latter will presumably speed things up a trifle. Progress will be achieved, from the bottom, through municipalities acquiring property at about the rate of £500m. a year, so that 'This process has but to continue long enough to ensure that every industry will pass under public control, and thus State Socialism will become an established fact, by a gradual process of easy transition'. (Hardie, p.28). From the top the work of building the millenium will commence with the protracted but inevitable achievement of a parliamentary majority.

The process—never clearly delineated—is an *inevitable* one and it is also a gradual one. No connection—logical or any other—is drawn between the two key concepts which are simply stated as self-evident facts. The underlying reason for the gradualist position is best stated in Jowett's essay when he writes that the socialist faces 'the necessity of carrying public opinion with him at every step [which] confines his power within very narrow limits'.[8] Further, both Headlam and Jowett stress that most people are indifferent to socialist appeals so that the work of converting people is necessarily a protracted one. But what does not seem to have been realised is that there may be a serious difficulty facing the gradualist who is also a socialist. The difficulty is that the more successful he is in introducing, or causing to be introduced, a series of reforms, the more likely is it that the amelioration the reforms effect will cause the system to become less and less burdensome to the majority of people. So far from gradually nudging Britain towards a socialist society it is arguable that the effect of the Labour Party has been to make the capitalist state a more flexible and viable institution than it might have been in the absence of that party.

The point concerning the unanticipated consequences of deliberate social amelioration can be illustrated by the list of tasks which Jowett insists a socialist municipality would undertake. As a matter of fact, most of them *are* now performed by municipalities, but it would be a bold man indeed who would claim that British local government is now socialist. Equally, it would be a niggardly and carping critic who failed to acknowledge the significant impact on local administration of socialists like Jowett. Similarly, although the 'Free Breakfast Table' is now not even a dream, the fact remains that most of the reforms required by Snowden are now common-place in *capitalist societies*. In this sense at least the gradualist, as represented in this volume, clearly failed to think out the implications of their reforms or, more likely, they underestimated the sheer flexibility and adaptibility of capitalism. But in so doing they joined the great majority of socialist thinkers, propagandists and politicians who interpreted every shortcoming of capitalism as evidence of decay and regarded every crisis as a 'historical turning-point'. Without some actual limits of reform—other than an assertion that there are limits—it seems plain that reformist socialism may be simply one of a number of possible techniques employed in the industrial society to integrate and domesticate the working class.[9] And, as this process proceeds, so the cry of 'crisis' and 'historical turning-point' becomes more desperate and unbelievable to the electoral majority.

A second characteristic displayed in the volume, which is quite closely connected with the optimism just noted, is a failure to think at all about what a socialist government would do first, second and third. That is to say, there is not a hint of priorities which derive from a theory or even a vision of how a socialist society would actually run. There is the assumption that it would consist of localised or nationalised industries—but not a hint about which ones would first be taken into public ownership nor yet a word about how they would actually operate. Writing of local government under socialism Jowett explains that 'In the Socialist City, officials instead of being scoffed at . . . will be respected', and Hardie writes approvingly of the 'engineers, architects, organisers, and managers who carry on the business'.[10] Other than these gnomic hints of bureaucratised society there is total silence about actual techniques of rule. And this is no mere cavil, since if it was not clear at the time to the authors then it is clear now that the absence of a market economy makes necessary a much more central role in the economy for public officials. In his essay Headlam—probably with the Webbs in mind—launches a barrage against those socialists 'whose ideal is the multiplication of licences and inspectors' and protests against 'the notion that Socialism consists in regulating and licensing and managing the lives of the people by a set of bureaucrats'.[11] However, it is one thing to protest, it is another to propose a non-bureaucratic alternative to the market as a rationing or allocating device in an industrial society or, indeed, in an under-developed society set upon rapid economic development.[12]

As much as any, it is this consideration which accounts for the failure of British socialism as an export-model to the developing world.[13] But another characteristic feature of British socialism also helps to account for its lack of success in this respect. This is, of course, the assumption that, economically, the system inherited by a socialist administration would be highly developed in at least the minimal sense that the problem of production had been solved and all that remained to be tackled was the problem of mal-distribution. 'The productive capacity of society', explained Jowett, 'is now so great that none need want and all are able to earn their livelihood and more'.[14] And the same spirit pervades Philip Snowden's meticulous exercise in social accounting which lacks even a glimmer of the more dynamic and enterprising *etatisme* or *dirigisme* which is so characteristic an aspect in modernising areas of socialism.[15] This assumption, that all major problems of distribution would be solved in a socialist system, meant that serious thinking about the actual problem of governing an actual society was neglected. Committed to gradualism and to reform, a Labour Government would necessarily come to power—if it came to power—in a dominantly capitalist society where (by current socialist definition) there would be unemployed people. And, as was discovered in 1924 and, more horrendously, in 1929–31, ritual incantations about socialism being the only permanent solution to the problem did not alleviate any distress. The party—or rather its leaders—had failed to think through the policy implications of its ideas.

This point has been taken up and developed by Robert Skidelsky who, whilst excoriating the incantatory nature of Labour Party socialism, makes the more important suggestion that Snowden's 'visionless orthodoxy'[16] came between the Labour Party and a serious consideration of non-orthodox financial measures to combat unemployment. Snowden's visionless orthodoxy was, of course, that of the classical British School of economics with the general proviso that 'private property is only permitted to be held or enjoyed by individuals so long as that private possession is not opposed to the general welfare, and so long as the community does not require the property or the income for public purposes'. (Snowden, p.4). The difficulty with such a formulation is that, quite literally, no reasonable person could object to it as a general statement. Hence, as a socialist Snowden adds that he would tax 'to secure such socially—created wealth as is now taken in Rent, Interest and Profit, and use this revenue for social reform purposes'. (Snowden, p.6). And as a general statement, although this lacks precision, it is quite clearly in the main stream of the socialist tradition. But, as Skidelsky points out, when the problem of the unemployed appeared in the 1920s it was not a matter of taxation but of deficit budgeting, public works to create employment, and possibly the adoption of protection. All were rejected out of hand, without, apparently, any hesitation by Snowden and by the Labour Party's top leadership echelon.

Rejection of innovation would have been one thing, but rejection on the grounds that, for example protective tariffs were anti-socialist, was quite another since, arguably, free-trade is the exact opposite of socialist control and manipulation of the national economy. As Tom Johnston, who was at least open-minded, later put it 'There were we as a party struggling to raise standards of living among the producing classes, urging factory acts and all manner of restrictions and penalties upon employers who underpaid labour and worked child labour for long hours, yet as a party committed to an extreme free trade in the importation of sweated goods'.[17] Yet, as a matter of fact, when Mosley and the ILP raised the possibility of tariffs in the 1920s there was an outcry against them in the Labour movement.[18] Similarly, in *Labour and the New Social Order* (1918), the Party had actually committed itself to arranging 'public works and the orders of the National Departments and local authorities in such a way as to maintain the aggregate demand for labour in the whole Kingdom (including that of capitalist employers) approximately at a uniform level from year to year'. Yet when the use of a revenue surplus in 1923 for public works was suggested, MacDonald insisted it went for debt reduction and in 1925 Snowden argued that 'the greater part of the money which has been spent in relief works ... has been from the economic view almost wholly wasted'.[19] They did not believe in public works financed by taxes and loans and they were simply not prepared to listen to the idea of financing such schemes by expanding bank credit.

The interesting problem here is *why* tariffs and manipulative monetary techniques were almost automatically ruled out by socialists in Britain. As much as anything it is likely that the absence of any thinking at all about monetary matters, a fear of being thought cranks in the 19th century mould (Attwood *etc.*), together with a belief that economics *was* a science, combine to explain the intellectual domination of Snowden. One should also not neglect the fact, quite obvious when comparing his contribution to that of the others in this volume, that he had a better, a clearer and a more precise mind that had his fellow authors. Again, it is not too difficult to suggest reasons why free trade had the pulling power it did for the Labour Party: it was *the* British radical posture of the nineteenth century, it did seem to make sense, and it was obviously compatible with Labour's internationalism.[20] National socialism appeared to have little emotional appeal—although Blatchford nearly gave it one—and the boisterous jingo nationalism of so many Labour leaders during the war might have given cause for thought.[21] Yet none was attempted by the leadership who stuck rigorously by free trade and internationalism and in this they were reinforced by the Liberal influx of 1914–22.[22]

And yet after all this is said one is still left with

a sense that it simply is not enough to explain why none of those challenging the leadership and its ideas were taken seriously. My own feeling is that these ideas were so loose and amorphous, so infinitely elastic, that they imposed no limits at all on the leadership—and equally failed to offer a basis of agreed principle from which the leadership could be attacked. But if their ideas were loose, it can equally be argued that the Party could therefore have accepted tariffs and deficit financing with little difficulty. They could, but the one man with a clear mind was adamantly against and there was no basis of principle from which he could be refuted. The Labour Party was not held together by a shared system of ideas or an ideology but rather by a limited tactical agreement between the unions and a number of parliamentary socialists, and the socialism of the party was emotional and rhetorical rather than structured and analytical. The basic agreement of the party was an emotional, not an intellectual one. MacDonald's adherence to general ideas which would not have been out of place in Burke appears not to have caused any inconvenience: 'As a mere machine it is somewhat inchoate. That, however, is rather a commendation than otherwise . . . that is the type of institution which yields best results. It goes not by logic and rigidity of its construction, but by an accumulation of precedent and the growth of a spirit and method appropriate to itself'. (MacDonald, p.78). It caused no more intellectual inconvenience than did Snowden's basically liberal economic thinking because the party was for most of the time more than willing to thrill to warm emotion and a warm revivalist rhetoric. Although Hardie was writing of the average man he might well have been writing of himself and the party leadership: 'With the speculative side of Socialism the average man with us has but small concern; it is its common sense which appeals to him'. (Hardie, p.34). And, during the debate in the mid-1920's, when, albeit clumsily, the leadership of the ILP did attempt to initiate a debate in the Labour Party on *Socialism in Our Time,* it was apparently sufficient for some of the leadership to expostulate about *'easie oozy asses'* whilst P.J. Dollan proudly proclaimed 'Your theorist is always missing opportunities because he has deluded himself that events must work out according to his theory ... The ILP is practicable and adaptable because it is idealistic and humanitarian rather than theoretical and abstract. The ILP is guided by its heart rather than by text-books'.[23] It would be very easy to fill a substantial volume with quotations from official ILP and Labour Party journals further illustrating this point but one more typical example will suffice: 'With Keir Hardie, their founder, the truest servants of the ILP have consistently mistrusted elaborate Socialist programmes and Athanasian Creeds replete with damnatory clauses ... the letter killeth, the spirit alone giveth life'.[24]

This almost blind devotion to the amorphous—it was not pragmatism or empiricism—was reinforced by the emotional quality of many socialists' attachment to socialism and to the Labour movement. The emotion reveals itself most clearly in Jowett's very moving, indeed, haunting final chapter when he described his Bradford street scene; and in every biography and autobiography of the Labour leadership the emotional quality of the cameraderie is stressed. The party was more than a party, it was a band of brothers: 'At the end of a long, inspiring speech, he would drop his voice and gently urge his listeners to play their part in the great cause. He [Snowden] would call on those who wished to join the party to walk to the front of the hall and sign the membership form. One by one they would come forward while, perhaps, the choir and the rest of the audience sang The Red Flag'.[25] In such an atmosphere criticism was easily taken as disloyalty and, although criticism of the leadership was frequent, it could usually be stemmed by an emotional appeal for loyalty and for patience. The Labour Party seems, at least up to 1931, to have been a party of hero-worshippers who drew their faith and based their politics on leaders rather than any firm ideological principle. Hence the odd and mixed bag of vegetarians, simple-lifers, folk-singers, tee-totallers and so on, who crowded into the party.

However, it is one thing to argue that intellectually the version of socialism advanced in this volume is not especially impressive, coherent or even convincing but quite another to suggest as Miliband does, that it contained any sort of 'inherent and inescapable consequences'.[26] It is not necessary to become involved in the largely sterile argument about the action-imperatives of more coherent and structured ideologies, but it is necessary to insist that in office even the most informed Marxists differ with each other. That is to say, there are ambiguities which may be seized upon by policy-makers to justify action more or less dictated by circumstances and events. Of course *some* courses of action may be ruled out by an ideological imperative, but looked at coldly it is very difficult indeed to claim that this possibility imposes a serious limitation on politicians claiming to be Communist, Nationalist, Socialist or whatever. Hence, the failure to tackle most problems in 1924 and 1929—31 with boldness and vigour had little, if anything, to do with the un-structured and incoherent ideology of Labourism since, literally, Labourism excludes nothing. With a basic policy which changed in no essential detail from that of the inter-war years, (except the incorporation of Keynesian monetary techniques) the Attlee government between 1945 and 1949 did, overall, act boldly and did introduce important social reforms.[27]

On the other hand, it is quite possible that, believing all problems would *somehow* be solved with the accession to power of a socialist government, the amorphous set of beliefs, inspirations, hopes and verbiage which made up the intellectual capital of English Labourism actually constituted a barrier to clear thinking. When it obtained office in 1924 the Labour Party was a propagandist party without even the vaguest idea of policy priorities: 'We are going to develop our own country, we are going to work it for all it is worth, to bring Labour into touch with God's natural endowments, and we are going to make the land blossom like a rose and contain houses and firesides, where there shall be happiness and contentment and glorious aspiration.'.[28] And it did not change in any essential respect by 1929 when, in the interim, there had been *some* thinking about socialist tactics, about deficit financing and about tariffs. The Labour leadership not merely failed to think, it was impervious to those who had bothered to think, and in so far as this failure was not a matter of temperament (MacDonald and Snowden) it is not unlikely that the necessity of thinking was obviated by socialist slogans and emotional rhetoric. For yet another type (Webb, and probably William Graham) socialism was not an action creed, it was an *explanation* of present discontents: 'There was something infinitely pathetic in the dead silence and intense interest with which they [Durham miners] listened to his [Webb's] long and carefully phrased descriptions of the causes of paralysed trade'.[29] And, as we have seen, they had no premonition at all of the problems set for an electorally successful socialist reformist party in a flexible capitalist society.[30] Hence, it is only in a very limited sense that one can accept the argument that the Labour Party's version of socialism—of which this volume is an excellent example—was in any serious way an impediment to radical action. What it did do, on the other hand, was to conceal the need for a system of policy priorities, prevented any systematic thought about administering an advanced capitalist society. More crucially than these, the rhetoric of socialism may well have prevented the party leadership from considering seriously the debate between Mosley and the ILP on raising and lowering bank rate, deficit financing, tariff and children's allowances. Again, the party leadership appears to have scorned—without carefully considering—the Lloyd George unemployment policy proposals of 1929 on the basis that they would not work ('madcap Finance') and that, anyway, they merely tinkered with the problem when what was needed was *Socialism*. [31]

Thus, the socialist rhetoric of the Labour Party so far from providing it with clear insight into its position as a reformist party in a capitalist society, actually prevented it from adopting the means—which in the 1920s might have involved some sort of amalgam or selection from Mosley, Hobson and Keynes—to make it an effective reformist party. Instead, the Labour leadership and followers were quite satisfied to wait for the inevitable failure of capitalism from amidst which would somehow blossom forth an equally inevitable socialist society. This bland optimism, which is perfectly characteristic of the essays here reprinted and of the other two in the series, was actually justified by the course that events took. As a matter of fact, the electoral vote of the party rose in every election but two between 1900 and 1950, and at every election between 1900 and 1945 (except 1931) the party increased the number of its MP's.

More crucial politically than even its optimism, the Labour Party did have the most enormous piece of political luck when the Liberal Party between 1910 and 1922 tore itself to pieces. And, not merely did the Liberal Party degenerate into a loose coalition of warring tribes, its leadership positively encouraged the aspirant Labour Party rather than trying to destroy it at birth. In 1914 it is broadly true that the 'Labour Parliamentary

Party still existed ... by Liberal indulgence—that is, because the Liberals deemed it advantageous to give Labour a free run against the Conservatives in certain seats'.[32] And, in concrete policy terms, the Labour Party could be distinguished only with difficulty from Liberals. Writing of a series of by-elections between 1911 and 1914 Douglas argues that 'The Liberal and Labour candidates do not seem actually to have disagreed on anything'.[33] There is not, in short, a scrap of evidence in this volume that the intellectual leaders of the Labour Party were provided with any sharp or incisive tool of analysis of the social and intellectual ferment which Britain underwent from about 1905. And when the ferment in the Labour movement on, for example, syndicalism, did actually occur the Labour Party leadership stood pat and rejected it root and branch. Nor yet does one find in the series the vaguest premonition that Britain was to undergo the combined shocks of the militant suffragettes, the Ulster crisis, the wave of strikes and, finally the Great War. That is to say, the Labour Party was not a serious rival to the Liberals electorally or politically, and intellectually there is no evidence at all that the socialism of the Labour Party gave it any special insight into the social crisis or the international situation. The extent to which the socialist creed of the Labour Party offered a clear insight into European social and political reality is vividly illustrated by Hardie's proud boast: 'In countries where the Socialist parties are a real influence in the councils of the Nation, the war spirit is suffering appreciable eclipse. It would, for instance, be a difficult task, and one yearly becoming more so, for the rulers of say, France and Germany, to again embroil these two nations in war with each other'. (Hardie, p.95). One cause of Hardie's death in 1915 was heart-break. And there is no evidence that purely in terms of social reform the Liberal government was unable to offer—and pass—legislation which undermined Labour's claim to a special political posture.[34] Indeed, as Wilson puts it, 'in 1914 . . . the social reform wing of the Liberal government was making the running. 'Advanced' thinkers were still looking to Liberalism to implement their ideas. And Labour had put forward no major policy items which the Liberal party was unable to implement'.[35]

Similarly, in Parliament—the chosen arena of the Labour leaders in which they were to demonstrate the viability of socialism—the Labour Party, following its real initial success in getting the union's immunity from civil actions for redress against strike techniques, was overshadowed by the Liberals. Not only was it overshadowed, but it was quite clear to everybody that this was the case, so that in 1909 Ben Tillet answered his own rhetorical question—'Is the Parliamentary Labour Party a Failure?'—with a decided affirmative.[36] In 1910 Hardie admitted that in Parliament the Labour Party 'almost ceased to count'.[37] And in 1912 Beatrice Webb lamented that 'The Labour MP's seem to be drifting in futility'.[38] By July 1914 the failure even to invite a Labour Party representative to the Buckingham Palace conference on the Ulster crisis simply confirmed their judgement. Dangerfield sums up the situation aptly: 'this

Labour contingent rapidly lost its terror. Even its twenty-nine professed socialists, those scandalous and impertinent revolutionaries, seemed prepared to vote with the Liberal majority, to wear frock coats, to attend royal garden parties, to become as time passed just a minor and far from militant act in the pantomime of Westminster'.[39] Yet, in none of the essays here reprinted is there the slightest premonition that such an eventuality was possible.

Thus, the Labour Party was not well poised in 1914 to displace the Liberals and as we have seen there was very little indeed to differentiate the 'advanced' Liberals from the Parliamentary Labour Party. Quite certainly, the proudest possession of the party—its socialism—was muted and not merely that, but it also failed to provide the party with a political perspective from which it could produce radical policies both distinctive and well thought out. But even this proved something of an advantage since, to all intents and purposes between 1910 and 1914 when, like Britian, the Liberal Party was riven by conflict, the Labour Party was publicly ignored and saved its political virginity by default. When war and the Coupon Coalition finally splintered the Liberals the optimism of the Labour Party was once again justified—something always *would* turn up. And to the limited extent that the party was involved in the government of the country during the war it was needed as a trade union organisation rather than as a party with a distinctive set of policies and ideas. That is to say, the party could not be associated with the governmental failures of pre-war Liberalism nor yet with the horror of the war—so it neither needed to nor did do much more than criticise and bide its distant but certain victory.

MacDonald's essay, *Labour and the Empire* is the most interesting departure from routine socialist polemic of the time about imperialism, in that it sees the Empire as a series of problems to be tackled rather than as an embarrassment to be got rid of. It might also be noticed that no attempt whatsoever is made to formulate a socialist policy for the Empire (whatever that would be) but simply to state what he understood to be 'the democratic principle of native administration'. This principle is 'to develop native civilisation on its own lines' and presumably, to foster the best of the indigenous traditions: to rule, that is to say, indirectly. (MacDonald, p.18). In opposition to this method of rule is the imperialistic method in which the native is directly ruled and has imposed upon him the metropolitan civilisation. MacDonald favours the former approach whilst insisting that 'the influence of the Labour Party on Imperial politics must be to democratise the personnel of the Imperial machine'. (MacDonald, p.27). Within the Empire, the self-governing states must each formulate their own internal policy yet, since each accepts a common imperial standard, there will be a measure of uniformity. Since we are not told what this standard is other than 'certain axioms regarding human liberty and the administration of justice' it is difficult to comment further, other than to call attention to the strong possibility that MacDonald was thinking primarily of a 'common racial policy'. (MacDonald, p.39).

So far, so vague, but MacDonald in this respect is no better or worse than numerous commentators who then, and now, attempt to square the circle of independence and uniformity on essential matters such as race and national interest. In writing of the non self-governing parts of the Empire, MacDonald gets into much deeper confusion. Regarding India he sets out a policy of non-intervention in native affairs and at the same time insists that 'our Government should win the confidence and assent of the people'. Just how the confidence of natives is to be won without intervention is not explained. It is not explained because a colonial policy of non-intervention and fostering native institutions is a contradiction in terms. Nor, more crucially, are we told who are the people—the masses, the emergent and Europeanised middle-class or the native rulers—whose confidence needs to be gained. The problem is, of course, that the interest of these groups often did and do not coincide. An inevitable consequence of this fact is that winning the approval of one group necessarily meant losing the support of another.

Again, although it does *sound* quite sensible to talk of fostering local traditions and to lament the errors of regarding 'the native as a Briton in the making' the sense is more apparent than real. For better or worse, colonialism necessarily results in a quite fundamental restructuring of indigenous life styles and, amongst the elite, of political, cultural and economic attitudes. Additionally, the social structure of the colonised society is profoundly changed by the mere presence of colonial officials, administrators, traders and so on. At the very least the incursors, even if they believe they are not interfering with native institutions, impact upon the local population as a reference group. Actually the impact of colonialists upon the social structure and psychology of the colonised was immense and irreversible so that MacDonald's lamentations about 'Britons in the making' are otiose. There is, and in 1907 there could be no way of going back to pre-colonised days before the Europeans so profoundly affected the areas he colonised. What one might have hoped for in an analysis by a socialist is some sense of the change that even well intentioned colonialism (if it be not a contradiction) wrought amongst the colonised. One might also have looked for concrete proposals concerning the training of local population at least to play a larger part in their own government; of this eventuality there is not a hint. Nor yet does MacDonald seriously discuss the possibility of ultimate independence for the smaller colonies and the steps a Labour administration would take to prepare for this outcome.

MacDonald's standpoint, then, is that of an intelligent and well-intentioned democrat who believed that the British colonies and Empire presented an opportunity to do some good in the world, and who had got beyond the idea of simply getting rid of them.[40] Very little that is distinctively socialist can be detected in any of his writings and certainly there is nothing novel in his contribution to this volume. The attempt to interest the Party in problems of Empire failed so that in the 1920s only about 20 Labour MPs were members of the Commonwealth Group in

Parliament and the level of thinking remained generally low. It was simply assumed that all tensions could be overcome by socialist parties winning electoral victories and forming governments in each independent nation. Socialists, it was thought, would be able to talk to one another in comradely tones and all artificial barriers to concord would soon collapse. One finds this blandly optimistic assumption in MacDonald's discussion of Empire and it was one which persisted for many years. Despite his interest, MacDonald in actual practice differed little, if at all, from his predecessors in office: 'When in 1924 Zaghlul asked MacDonald to remove British troops and British advisors, to annul British control over Egypt's external relations and the British claim to protect foreigners and minorities, and to abandon the British claim to share in any way in protecting the Suez Canal, he got an answer singularly free of Radical bias'.[41]

Thus, the Labour Party was characterised by an extremely loose collection of ideas, an almost impenetrable optimism and, happily for its continued and growing stature in British politics, a rival party which an unfortunate concatenation of events and personal dislikes conspired to almost destroy. There was never any serious question that the Labour Party could set its *distinctive* mark on the British political system since it had no distinctive mark to set. And if it had had such a distinctive set of ideas and policies there is little reason to believe it would have been given the opportunity to implement them. One very significant consequence of the ideas contained in this volume is that they enabled or caused the pre-1914 war generation of Labour leaders to misunderstand or not examine at all the collection of ideas whose adoption *might* have led to a dynamic and politically innovative Labour Government in 1929. As it was, the Government assumed office with no policy at all to tackle the endemic unemployment problem nor to stem the economic blizzard other than to postpone solutions until the left-wing equivalent of the Greek Kalends—the arrival of Socialism.

NOTES

The place of publication is London, unless otherwise stated

[1] R. Miliband, *Parliamentary Socialism* (1964) p.144.

[2] In *New Leader,* 12th December 1930.

[3] R.W. Lyman, *The First Labour Government* (1957) p.215 writes that in imperial affairs: 'Faced with real problems of Imperial policy, Ministers found new virtues in policies they would have denounced, in Opposition, as Tory Imperialism'.

[4] Ethel Snowden, *The Socialist Woman,* p.1.

[5] Ibid., p.16.

[6] As a *Liberal* song of 1910 put it 'Why should we be beggars with the ballot in our hand?' Cited in R. Douglas, *The History of the Liberal Party, 1895—1970* (1971) p.52.

[7] Frederick W. Jowett, *The Socialist and the City,* p.5. Note here again the assumption that socialism is simply all good things.

[8] Frederick W. Jowett, *The Socialist and the City,* p.3.

[9] See T.H. Marshall, *Sociology at the Crossroads* (1963) pp.67—127 and pp.289—308.

[10] Frederick W. Jowett, *The Socialist and the City,* p.17.

[11] Stewart D. Headlam, *The Socialist's Church,* pp.55 and 53.

[12] See E. Berg, 'Socialism and Economic Development in Tropical Africa', *Quarterly Journal of Economics,* November 1965.

[13] See J. Kautsky, *Political Change in Underdeveloped Countries: Nationalism and Communism* (New York, 1962) pp.1—115.

[14] Frederick W. Jowett, *The Socialist and the City,* p.66.

[15] See for example W.H. Friedland and C.G. Rosberg, *African Socialism* (Stanford, 1964) pp.1—34.

[16] R. Skidelsky, *Politicians and the Slump* (1967) p.38.

[17] Tom Johnston, *Memories* (1952) p.53.

[18] See Robert E. Dowse, *Left in the Centre* (1966) pp.130–51.

[19] Cited in K.J. Hancock, 'The Reduction of Unemployment as a Problem of Public Policy, 1920–29', *Economic History Review*, December 1962.

[20] The Labour leadership, after the Treaty of Versailles, believed that only a sane *foreign* policy—admitting Germany to the League, abolition of reparations and bringing Russia more into the comity of nations—would help solve the problem of unemployment in Britain; see Robert E. Dowse, 'The Independent Labour Party and Foreign Politics, 1918–1923', *International Review of Labour History*, 7, 1962, pt.1.

[21] Headlam was a member of the Socialist National Defence Committee, formed in April 1915 to oppose the socialist anti-war movement. In 1916 the Committee became the British Worker's National League devoted to military victory and advocating the take-over by Britain of the German colonies.

[22] See Robert E. Dowse, 'The Entry of Liberals Into the Labour Party 1910–1920', *Yorkshire Bulletin of Economic and Social Research*, November 1961.

[23] In *Socialist Review*, 28, May 1927.

[24] *Labour Leader*, 7 April 1921. L. Thompson, *The Enthusiasts: A Biography of John and Katherine Bruce Glasier* (1971) is an especially rich source of this type of thinking and language. See G. Ditz, 'Utopian Symbol in the History of the British Labour Party', *British Journal of Sociology*, 17, July 1966.

[25] C. Cross, *Philip Snowden*, (1966) p.37.

[26] Miliband, op.cit., p.144.

[27] The ideology of the Swedish Social Democratic Labour Party was marginally more coherent than that of the British Labour Party yet it adopted Keynesian ideas in the early 1930s with no trouble and considerable electoral success.

[28] J.R. MacDonald in *Daily Herald*, 2 November 1923.

[29] M. Cole (ed), *Beatrice Webb's Diaries, 1912–1924* (1952) p.219. Yet it should be stressed that Webb *did* believe in governmental intervention to maintain high levels of employment, and this belief was actually enshrined in *Labour and the New Social Order*.

[30] The problem is, of course, that the advanced capitalist society is quite capable of absorbing and actually benefitting from the electoral and political success of a reformist socialist party, whilst there is scant evidence that more 'advanced' socialist parties in such societies are well-poised for electoral victory.

[31] This was a standard gambit of men like Snowden who, in 1927, had the temerity to attack the ILP Living Wage policy as 'mere Liberalism', *New Leader*, 27 April 1927.

[32] Trevor Wilson, *The Downfall of the Liberal Party, 1914–1935* (Fontana edition, 1968) p.19. A standard account of the 1903 MacDonald–Gladstone secret agreement concludes, 'in the actual circumstances of January 1906 it was clearly the Labour candidates who were the principal beneficiaries', F. Bealey and H. Pelling, *Labour and Politics, 1900–1906* (1958) p.288.

[33] Douglas, op.cit., p.87.

[34] H. Pelling, *Popular Politics and Society in Late Victorian Britain,* (1968) p.163.

[35] Wilson, op.cit., p.19.

[36] This was the title of a pamphlet Tillet published which roundly criticised the performance of the party in Parliament.

[37] *ILP Annual Report,* 1910, p.58.

[38] Webb Diaries, op.cit., p.6.

[39] George Dangerfield, *The Strange Death of Liberal England,* (Paladin edition, 1970) p.24.

[40] See A.P. Thornton, *The Imperial Idea and its Enemies,* (1966) ch.1.

[41] Ibid., p.248; Lyman, op.cit., p.214, 'Regarding India ... the Labour Government's policy was not easy to distinguish from that of the Tories'.

THE LABOUR IDEAL

FROM SERFDOM TO SOCIALISM

FROM SERFDOM TO SOCIALISM

BY

J. KEIR HARDIE, M.P.

LONDON: GEORGE ALLEN
156, CHARING CROSS ROAD
1907

Printed by BALLANTYNE, HANSON & CO.
At the Ballantyne Press, Edinburgh

Publisher's Note

Socialism being one of the most important subjects of to-day, its opponents and supporters alike need a frank, precise, and absolutely authentic account of its aim and methods. The Publisher wishes by means of this series to put clearly before the public a complete conspectus of the present policy of the English Socialists and the Independent Labour Party. To ensure authority and precision, arrangements have been made with the acknowledged leaders, in action and thought, of the new movement to contribute volumes to the " Labour Ideal " series on those branches of Socialism with which they are particularly connected.

The Publisher does not, of course, hold himself responsible for the opinions of the writers.

FOREWORD

THE attitude of multitudes of people towards Socialism is that of the man who could not see the wood for the trees. They are so engrossed in the contemplation of petty details that they never get even a remote glimpse of the great unifying principle underlying Socialism. Who is to blacken the boots and do the scavenging? What about the dangerous and disagreeable occupations such as mining and seafaring? How are we going to secure that each does his fair share and no more of the work, and receive his fair share and no more of the resultant wealth? How is genius to be rewarded under Socialism, and how is Art to be recognised? Since all are to be equal, what is to become of the man with exceptional ability? Is he to be specially rewarded? If not, what incentive will there be to his putting forth his special abilities, and if he is, what becomes of the promised equality?

These and a hundred and one others of a like kind are the objections with which the Socialist advocate is continually being met. Unless he can give a detailed and circumstantial explanation of how each and every one of these difficulties is to be overcome, his opponent goes away exulting in the belief that he has demolished the case for Socialism. With great respect I venture to submit that none of these things at all affect the question at issue, which is whether Socialism represents a desirable set of principles which, if acted upon, would materially lessen the burden of human woe and tend to the further development and improvement of the human race. If it be admitted that such results would follow the adoption of Socialism, then the adaptation of means to realise that end should present but few, and those easily overcome, difficulties. It is only by leaving out all allowance for common sense that the difficulties appear to be great and insuperable.

It is not within the scope of my intention in writing this little brochure to enter into an elaborate disquisition on the historical basis of Socialism, or to embody its economic theories and principles in a learned treatise.   These things have been done by other and more competent hands.   The moving Why which guides me is the belief I have of the need there is of a brief unadorned statement of the case for Socialism, easily understandable by plain folk, and in which incidentally some of the objections of our opponents may be met and some of the difficulties in the way of the earnest seeker after truth may be removed.   It has been written, literally, in the odd half-hours of a busy period in a life crowded with work. Whilst I have sought to buttress my opinions by quotations from writers of recognised authority, I do not in any way seek to shelter myself behind them.   For the opinions expressed I hold myself alone responsible, and desire it to be clearly understood that no one else is committed by them.   I have provided a list of works at the end of the book which may be read by those who desire to learn more about Socialism and the issues which it raises.   J. K. H.

1st January 1907.

b

CONTENTS

CHAP.   PAGE

I. BASIC PRINCIPLES I

II. MUNICIPAL SOCIALISM II

III. SOCIALISM AND THE STATE . . . 23

IV. SOCIALISM AND CHRISTIANITY . . . 35

V. SOCIALISM AND THE WORKER . . . 45

VI. SOCIALISM AND THE WOMAN QUESTION . 61

VII. FROM SERFDOM TO SOCIALISM . . . 71

VIII. SUMMARY AND CONCLUSION . . . 87

APPENDIX 109

BIBLIOGRAPHY 129

          . . . To fight,
Not in red coats against our brother man,
The pawns of Empire, or a despot's will,
But in grey lines of sober Brotherhood
Against the flaunting evils of the world,
The Cruelty that fastens on men's lives,
The dread brutality that hedges earth.

Come, ye that listen, rise and gird your swords,
Win back the fields of England for the poor,
Give roses to your children's fading cheeks,
And to the hearts of women hope again,
Bring back content unto the lives of men.

FROM SERFDOM TO SOCIALISM

CHAPTER I

BASIC PRINCIPLES

SOCIALISM is much more than either a political creed or an economic dogma.   It presents to the modern world a new conception of society and a new basis upon which to build up the life of the individual and of the State. Hitherto we have been accustomed to assume that because in the lower phases of life we witness what appears to be a continual struggle for existence, with the barriers of want ever pressing against the increasing multitudes of animals and plants requiring support, that these same conditions must also necessarily apply to human existence.   Nature red in tooth and claw, may be a faithful description of the conditions which accompany the struggle for life in the depth of the jungle— although even this is now open to grave doubt

—but, admitting for the moment for the sake of argument that such is the case, that does not seem to give any justification for reason-endowed man allowing himself to be guided in his organisation of society by the laws which govern the life of the unreasoning brute. For what purpose has man been endowed with reason if not to enable him to rise above the brute creation, not merely in his organisation of the means of procuring food, but also in the relation of the individual towards his fellows? If the law of the jungle is to be his rule of life, what becomes of his claim to be a religious being endowed with an immortal soul?

To the Socialist the community represents a huge family organisation in which the strong should employ their gifts in promoting the weal of all, instead of using their strength for their own personal aggrandisement. In like manner the community of States which compose the world, and making full allowance for the differences of environment, of tradition, and of evolution, he regards as a great comity which should be co-operating for the elevation of the race. Believing these things, the Socialists of all lands are working for their realisation. Herbert Spencer has pointed out that Altruism—each for all and all for each—is

but the highest form of enlightened selfishness.
He and the school of Individualists to which
he belonged, and which still has its representatives, although a dwindling band, differed from
the Socialist only in the method by which he
sought to achieve the end which both have
in common, the freedom of the individual. To
Spencer any interference with the freedom
of individual action seemed baneful. He
conceived society as a collection of units,
each one struggling to make the best of his
individual life and thus finding the niche in
life which he was intended to occupy, whilst
learning by experience that co-operation and
not competition is the only true basis upon
which progress can be built. But the co-
operation must be free and voluntary, and not
imposed from without by any law other than
that of enlightened self-interest. This conception of the evolution of society has great
attractions, but it presupposes certain conditions which do not exist. The judge, the soldier,
and the policeman are violations of the basic
law upon which Spencer founded his thesis.
Restraint is restraint whether it be a Factory
Act or a Peace Preservation Act, and if the
State has no right to interfere to protect the
poor struggling against circumstances over
which they have no control in the industrial

world, it is difficult to see why the same
State should be considered a beneficent
agency when called in to protect the property
of the rich against an infuriated mob of
starving people. If the poor are to be left
to struggle for existence unaided by the State,
then why not the rich? If it be replied that
the State is part of the environment which the
owners of property have evolved for their own
protection, the obvious answer is that so soon
as the working-class succeed in capturing
and controlling the machinery of the State it
will then also become part of their natural
environment. The law of evolution leaves
no doubt on the point, that there comes a
time when the individual, unable to struggle
longer against overwhelming odds, succumbs,
and that whole species have thus disappeared
from the animal and vegetable worlds. It is
no reply in this connection to say that higher
forms of life have taken their place. If it
could be shown that the great Trust magnate
or the great Aristocratic landowner, apart
from the advantages of his inherited wealth,
was a more highly developed species of
humanity than the poor struggling sempstress
or the unemployed docker, then there might
be some justification for allowing the docker
and the sempstress as the representatives of

a weaker class to die out in order to enable the more highly developed creature to survive; but one moment's reflection will show that the alleged superiority of the landowner or the Trust magnate rests on one fact alone, namely, that he owns certain material possessions, usually inherited, which enable him to dictate the terms upon which his less fortunate fellow-creatures shall be permitted to live. And really in the end he is more dependent upon them than they on him. Were they to die out, he also would die with them, he being but a parasite whose life is dependent upon their continued existence; whereas, his disappearance as a class would free the other classes from a great weight with which they are now burdened, and thus leave them much better equipped for the battle of life. If, then, all men are to be free, in the Individualistic sense of that term, then an indispensable preliminary is the abolition of the State and the free grouping together of sections of the community according to their respective affinities. Men like Tolstoy and Kropotkin openly advocate a revolutionary change of this kind, and in this they are at least consistent. When brought face to face with the probable outcome of their own theories, however, they admit that in place of the State there would grow up great Co-operative organisations, and that these would require to work together for mutual aid and support, and would necessarily require rules and regulations for their guidance, so that in the end we should get back to pretty much the existing organisation, only under another guise. The State as we know it is a growth born of the needs of the times, and is continually adapting itself to meet the changing influence which controls its working. The assumption that under the voluntary Co-operative organisation plan each individual would be free either to submit or not as he pleased to the will of the majority, is a pure fallacy. Under the State now each individual is free to act as he pleases provided he is willing to take the consequences. Hunger is a much more potent weapon than any form of penal enactment for bringing an insubordinate member of the community to subjection, and under any conceivable form of voluntary co-operation the individual who put himself in opposition to the clearly expressed will of his fellows would fare no better than he does at present. The individualistic conception of the State as some external authority exercising a malign influence upon the life of the community is a travesty of fact. The State is that form of organised society which has evolved through the process of the ages, and represents the aptitude for freedom and self-government to which any people has attained. The policeman and the soldier, for example, who are at the call of the landlord or the employer when tenant or workman becomes turbulent, exist by the will and under the express authority of those same tenants and workmen, who constitute a preponderating majority in the State, and without whose consent neither soldier nor policeman could continue to exist. It is their toil which pays for their maintenance; it is from their ranks that they are drawn; and it is their votes which create the Parliament which creates the policeman and the soldier. The Socialist therefore, recognising that the State is but the expression of the will of the people, accepts it as an existing fact, and seeks by means of the education of the electorate to change the conception upon which the State at present rests and the functions which it exercises. Theoretically, the State exists to protect life and property: in fact, the modern State exists primarily to protect property, and will destroy life as freely as it is destroyed either in the caverns of the ocean or the depths of the forest rather than allow property to be forcibly interfered with in the slightest degree.

This, however, is but natural when we remember that in the past only the propertied classes had any real influence in the moulding of the State. From the dawn of history we get glimpses of the toiling multitude slowly emerging from serfdom. We see one section after another painfully winning its way into political recognition, but always as the owners of property. Hence the fact that the State is primarily concerned with the preservation of the rights of property. The aristocrat as the great war lord, the yeoman as his captain, the trading and commercial classes, and the great barons of finance have all in turn succeeded in asserting themselves and impressing their will upon the State. As each of these sections have won recognition for themselves they have recognised that they had a common interest with all the rest in keeping the propertyless mass of the common people in subjection, and have joined forces for that purpose. Obviously the surest method for keeping the masses in subjection to their lords in the olden time was to make the land private property. A landless peasantry could have no rights.

Latter years have seen the Capitalist and Commercial classes successfully winning their way to influence and power in the councils of the nation, and they in turn have surrounded

their particular form of property—Capital—
with the odour of sanctity and reduced the
artisan to the same dependent position as
the landless peasant. No law can give freedom to a people which is dependent upon
some power or authority outside themselves
for the necessaries of life. The owners of
the means of life can dictate the terms upon
which all who are not owners are to be
permitted to live. This is the great new fact
which Socialists are bringing to the front.
Socialism says to the worker, It is not the
State which holds you in bondage, it is the
private monopoly of those means of life without which you cannot live, and until you make
these means of life the common property and
inheritance of all you can never hope to escape
from your bondage. The economic object of
Socialism, therefore, is to make land and industrial capital common property, and to
cease to produce for the profit of the landlord and the capitalist and to begin to produce
for the use of the community.

The disinherited and propertyless people are
learning that Socialism and freedom "gang
thegither," and will use the State as the means
whereby property, and the freedom which
its possession ensures, shall become the common inheritance of every citizen.

This change in the ownership of land and capital and in the object of production, however, is merely the medium through which it is hoped the Socialist spirit will find expression. Socialism implies the inherent equality of all human beings. It does not assume that all are alike, but only that all are equal. Holding this to be true of individuals, the Socialist applies it also to races. Only by a full and unqualified recognition of this claim can peace be restored to the world. Socialism implies brotherhood, and brotherhood implies a living recognition of the fact that the duty of the strong is not to hold the weak in subjection, but to assist them to rise higher and ever higher in the scale of humanity, and that this cannot be done by trampling upon and exploiting their weakness but by caring for them and showing them the better way.

CHAPTER II

SOCIALISM does not propose to abolish land or capital. Only a genius could have thought of this as an objection to Socialism. Socialism proposes to abolish capitalism and landlordism. The landlord, *qua* landlord, performs no function in the economy of industry or of food production. He is a rent receiver; that, and nothing more. Were the landlord to be abolished, the soil and the people who till it would still remain, and the disappearance of the landowner would pass almost unnoticed. So too with the capitalist. I do not refer to the man who manages his own business; he is a business manager, not a capitalist. By capitalist, I mean the investor who puts his money into a concern and draws profits therefrom without participating in the organisation or management of the business. Were all these to disappear in the night, leaving no trace behind, nothing would be changed. The capital would remain; the engineers, architects, organisers, and managers who carry on the businesses would all remain also, and could just as well and as profitably be employed by society as they now are by the private capitalist. This point has been so well expressed in a recent magazine article by Mr. G. Balfour Browne, a King's Counsel of high standing, that I make no apology for quoting his words :—

"Socialism, as we have seen," he says, "is no longer a war against capital, for it recognises that no work can be done without an expensive equipment. Before we can put the poor to work we must have raw material, we must have the machinery which with the help of labour is to produce the finished article : but it is a war against the holding of capital in private hands, and the payment of profits to those who hold the capital, instead of to the State which ought to hold the capital. Take a simple illustration. If a Gas Company exists in a town, it supplies gas to those who require that kind of illuminant, and the persons who use the gas are benefited thereby, for the company can produce and sell gas much more cheaply than the individuals could supply themselves. But the company spends its money not to benefit the consumer, but to secure what is called a return on its capital. . . . This profit comes out of the pockets of the consumers of gas, and is regarded by the Socialists in the light of a tax. One thing is certain, and that is, that if the capital for the enterprise had been raised by the municipal corporation of the town, and the undertaking had been carried on as efficiently in the hands of the corporation as in the hands of the company, the profits resulting from the manufacture and distribution of gas might have gone into the public purse and been applied by the town to the reduction of rates, or they might have been given to the consumers of gas by reduction of the price of gas. In either of these events the public would have been the gainers, and the only losers would have been the shareholders in the company, who would not have found a profitable investment for their money.

" Now a precisely similar course of reasoning is applicable to any private ownership. Presumably a man holds land in order that he may receive the profits. A manufactory is erected with a view to gain ; a railway is made by shareholders in order that they may reap a harvest of profit. Ships are sailed, banks established with the same object in view. If all these enterprises are profitable in the hands of private enterprise, it is obvious that the gains of such undertakings find their way into private pockets, and come out of the pockets of the public who use the land, who buy the manufactured article, who travel on the railway, who pay the freight, or who borrow from the bank. The desire of the Labourist is that all these profits should find their way into the public purse, and be disbursed for the benefit of the public. The foundation of this claim to appropriate all these means of production, distribution, and exchange is that the profits have not been created by the capitalist, but by the workmen, and consequently they belong to Labour and not to wealth.

"But the argument goes further. It is pointed out that the tax which is levied every year by the landowner in the form of rent for farms, or ground-rent for 'stands' in cities, the interest on the public debt, the profits upon such enterprises as those we have referred to, as they have to be paid by the people, have to be in the first instance earned by the people, and that this system is equivalent to the *corvée*, for the workman has to work about one-third of his whole time for himself and his family, and about two-thirds of his whole time to pay these taxes to the rich. It is true that the workman would even in the case of a Collectivist State have to toil a portion of his time to pay rent, but the rent would go to the State, and therefore belong to him. He might have to work to pay interest on the public debt, but it would be a debt that had been incurred by him, and not, as our existing debt is, a debt incurred by capitalists in the interests of capital. He might have to labour to replace machinery, and even to pay a sinking fund; but the machinery would be his own, and he and his class would be the beneficiaries when the sinking fund had paid off the capital cost of the establishment. In this way, it is argued that under the present system the wage-earner is not his own property. For two-thirds of his time he is a slave, labouring not for himself but for others, and Socialism is to emancipate him and let men in future own their own bodies and souls." [1]

This, coming as it does from an avowed opponent of Socialism, shows the common sense side of the movement. If the Community, through its elected representative institutions, national and municipal, can dispense with the private capitalist and landowner in the matter of houses, gas, water, electricity, tramways, insurance, why not also in such other essentials of life as bread, clothing, and furniture ? If the State can build battleships and make swords, why not also trading ships and ploughshares ? Since the State conveys letters and parcels and telegrams, why not also coal and wool and grain ? And if the State insists upon owning telegraph lines, why not also railway lines ? And if the railways, why not the coal mines from whence the power is drawn which sets the engines in motion ? And if the coal mines, why not the ironworks and engineering shops in which the raw materials for the rails and the engines and the trucks are produced and fashioned into shape ? When the

[1] Article in *National Review* for November 1906.

State enters upon business in any department there is no logical halting-place short of complete State Socialism, and the further extension of its trading activities is purely a question of utility. Attempts to draw imaginary lines of demarcation between what is properly State and what private spheres of business influence, always break down hopelessly when put to the test of principle. If water be a necessity of life, a common requirement of all, and therefore its supply a proper undertaking for the municipality, then so also is bread. Time was when water was not supplied through a monopoly granted either to a company or a municipality, as is now almost universally the case, and in those days each individual had to arrange for a supply as best he could. Experience showed, however, that the public convenience and the public health would both be gainers by making the supply of water a public concern, and no one nowadays challenges the wisdom of this step. Municipal milk depots are now, and for similar reasons, becoming common, and the beneficial results, on the health of infants especially, are such as to make the extension of this form of municipal trading a certainty.

In this connection it is interesting to recall the fact that municipalities in thus extending the sphere of their activities are but reverting to a sound rule of self-government of an earlier period. One reason for the extraordinary growth of cities in the Middle Ages was not merely that life was more secure within than without their walls, but also that the interests and welfare of the citizens were more carefully safeguarded. In very ancient times, in the palmy days that is to say of Greece and Rome, something closely akin to Communism seems to have obtained. In Sparta there were not only common lands, but also a common table, whilst dogs and horses were practically common property also. The common tables were kept supplied by each citizen contributing an equal quota. Attendance at them was compulsory, and it was an offence for any one to " fatten like voracious animals in private." Sparta, which kept its Communism almost to the end, was also the Republic from which came the immortal heroes who made the pass of Thermopylæ one of the great inspirations of the world. When, however, Communism was abandoned, and individuals began to amass fortunes, decay set in and Greece became a tributary to Rome. So long as the lands of Rome remained common property, power and prosperity belonged to the people. Wealth derived from conquered territories led to the growth of a wealthy class who made inroads upon old customs, and finally converted the public lands into large private estates and reduced the peasantry to bondage and beggary, and Rome fell. True, it may be alleged that in both these instances the benefits of communal property were confined to the comparatively few free citizens, and that the great army of working slaves, who had no rights, did not share in its benefits. This, however, in no way affects my argument, which is that with the growth of Capitalistic Individualism, and the accumulation of large fortunes, dry rot sets in, patriotism departs, and ruin overtakes the erstwhile most powerful peoples.

Coming nearer to our own times, we have still more evidence of a fairly well-developed communal life producing marvellous results. The great cities of the Middle Ages, now the show places of the world, were all built at a time when every private interest was held in subordination to the common weal. There were, primarily the Guilds, the trade unions of the period, in which the craftsmen were banded together for mutual aid and support. These undertook and carried through great public works, churches, town halls, bridges, and the like under the direct authorisation of the Town Council. There were town lands on which the town shepherds attended to the flocks and herds of their fellow-citizens. The markets, bridges, houses, and public buildings were nearly all communal property. So were the harbours and quays, and, sometimes at least, the vessels lying in them. But the town went much further than this in its care for the citizens. One of the fundamental principles of city government, as stated by one investigator, was to provide for "the common first food and lodging of poor and rich alike." It was a crime, punishable sometimes by death, to "forestall" the market. That is to say, any one going outside the city walls, or even beyond the boundaries of the market place, to purchase food, fuel, or raiment on terms and conditions not open to every citizen, was guilty of committing a felonious act. The citizen purchasing for his own use had the first claim upon the market, and after him the retail tradesman. It was another offence to buy goods wholesale in order to sell to retail traders. Middlemen were accounted no better than the common cutpurse, and treated accordingly. Any one discovered trying to create a corner in food was deemed a greater scourge than the highway robber, and incurred the death penalty for his pains. When food was scarce it had to be shared, each receiving according to his needs, whilst even in times of plenty prices were fixed by town officials, the "Mayor and two discreet men," so as to ensure that no more than an honest profit would be exacted. But even this does not exhaust the activities of the mediæval town. There is documentary evidence extant to show that during the sixteenth century the town itself did the buying and distributing of food and fuel, probably, though not always, through the Trade Guilds. From London to Thurso, and from Neath to Waterford, this practice seems to have been common. The town saw that the goods made and sold were honest in workmanship and material, and that the prices charged the consumer were fair. Finally, the town provided rational amusement for the people in the form of concerts, plays, games, and the like. The men of these periods do not appear to have suffered either in character or public spirit from all this Socialist coddling. The cathedrals of our own and other lands, or such of them as remain, testify to the spirit of beauty which animated them as well as to the enduring quality of their craftsmanship. The ruined castles are monuments to their public spirit, since it was they who overthrew the war barons of that age and helped to give freedom to the land serfs. They kept kings at bay and refused to pay taxes in the levying of which they had had no say, and thus led to Parliament being formed. They were the real custodians and champions of freedom, largely because their civic institutions protected the liberty of each individual.

The modern Municipal Socialist is thus seen to be no rash innovator, venturing into an unknown sphere of public work, but only reverting back to a type of which he need not be ashamed. When he seeks to bring the necessaries as well as the conveniences of life under public ownership and control, he is but seeking to resuscitate a phase of British life which produced great and good results in the past. When the produce of the Village Commune was sold direct to the consumer in the municipal market of the neighbouring town, there was such prosperity and fulness of life in our country as it has not known since, and it was only when this condition of things and all that it stood for was destroyed by the intrigues of kings and their allies that poverty and poor laws came into being. The modern Socialist has the further assurance that the causes which led to the overthrow of such Communism as there was in town and country are not likely to operate again. Commercialism, with the form of Individualism which it carried with it, has now run its course and exhausted itself. It is now the receding, not the advancing power. The trend of the age is away from the arid realm in which Mammonism has so long held sway, and the tide of opinion is advancing strongly in the direction of a more human epoch. Wearied with its vain efforts to find happiness in money-making, mankind is now returning to its older and wiser self and is seeking to find in service that content and peace of mind which selfishness has failed to give.

CHAPTER III

SOCIALISM AND THE STATE

THE State, as already stated, is what its people make it. Its institutions are necessarily shaped to further and protect the interests of the dominant influence. Whilst a landed nobility reigned supreme, the interests of that class were the one concern of the State. Subsequently with the growth of a commercial and trading class, which, when it became strong enough, insisted upon sharing the power of the State with the landed aristocracy, many of the old laws passed by the landlords in restraint of trade were modified. Now that the working-class is the dominant power, potentially at least, it logically and inevitably follows that that class will also endeavour to so influence the State as to make it protect their interests. As the political education of the working-class progresses, and they begin to realise what are the true functions of the State, their power will be exerted in an increasing degree in the direction of transforming the State from a property-preserving to a life-preserving institution. The fundamental fact which the working-class is beginning to recognise is that property, or at least its possession, is power. This is an axiom which admits of no contradiction. So long as property, using the term to mean land and capital, is in the hands of a small class, the rest of the people are necessarily dependent upon that class. A Democracy, therefore, has no option but to seek to transform these forms of property, together with the power inherent in them, from private to public possession. Opinion may differ as to the methods to be pursued in bringing about the change, but concerning its necessity there are no two opinions in the working-class movement. When land and capital are the common property of all the people class distinctions, as we know them at present, will no longer exist. The Mind will then be the standard by which a man's place among his fellows will be determined.

Socialist tactics have been as fruitful a cause of controversy as Socialism itself. In the early stages of the movement, at a time when the franchise was limited to the propertied classes and the working-class exercised practically no influence in the councils of the nation, the Socialist saw no means by which his purpose could be achieved save by revolution. The early, and in many respects the greatest, writers on Socialism frankly proclaimed armed revolution as being an essential part of their Socialist theories. They pictured the wealthy growing wealthier and the poor poorer, until a moment when, their poverty and suffering unendurable, the working-class would rise in wild revolt and overthrow the system which oppressed them. The advocates of this school, of whom some few still remain, did not admit the possibility of Socialism being gradually incorporated into the life of the nation. For a number of years the late William Morris, the greatest man whom the Socialist movement has yet claimed in this country, held and openly preached this doctrine of cataclysmic upheaval and sudden overthrow of the ruling classes, although in the closing years of his life he frankly threw it over. By this school of thinkers reforms for the amelioration of the lot of the people were anathematised as the wiles of the enemy to withdraw their attention from Socialism and make them contented with their lot as wage slaves. Let the Social sore bleed, they said, in effect, that all its ghastly horror may be brought home to the conscience of the nation; and the more miserable the lot of the workers the sooner would the revolution come. These tactics, however, have now been openly abandoned by the Socialist leaders in every constitutionally governed country. In Germany more social reforms for the benefit of the working-class have been enacted by the State than in any country in Europe, and it is in Germany where Socialism has made, and continues to make, greatest progress. France makes a good second in both respects. It is the intelligent fairly well-off artisan in Great Britain who responds most readily to the Socialist appeal, and it is the slum vote which the Socialist candidate fears most. In order to be effectually discontented, said Thorold Rogers, a people must be prosperous : when misery revolts it strikes blindly, and is generally restrained.

The modern Socialist recognises that a people depressed, weakened, and enervated by poverty and toil are more likely to sink into a nation of spiritless serfs than to rise in revolt against their lot. Experience also has shown that just in proportion as the lot of the worker is improved and his intelligence quickened, so does he become discontented and anxious for still further improvement. This is in accordance with all we know of the law of progress, and finds illustration on every hand. Further, it is now recognised that the progress of an idea in time influences even those whose interests are threatened by its success. No better illustration of this could be found than that supplied by the progress of the agitation against landlordism in Ireland. For generations the landlords of that country waged a relentless and unceasing war against its people. So bad did the condition of the peasantry become, that at length the State intervened to prevent their being altogether exterminated. Fair rents, fixity of tenure, and compensation for improvement gave the peasants of Ireland a new hope, and as that hope grew so did their strength increase and their agitation develop until there came a time at the beginning of the present century when the landlord class frankly admitted that dual control was no longer possible, and their one concern came to be, what were the best terms for themselves upon which it could be brought to an end ? In like manner it is conceivable that the transference of industries from private hands to the State will be a gradual and peaceful process. Already, in fact, the process has advanced to a considerable stage. The property held and worked and controlled by municipalities already exceeds £500,000,000 sterling in value, and is being added to yearly. This process has but to continue long enough to ensure that every industry will pass under public control, and thus State Socialism will become an accomplished fact, by a gradual process of easy transition.

A recognition of this fact has brought about a complete change in Socialist tactics. With the enfranchisement of the masses it is recognised that the ballot is much more effective than the barricade. The mere weight of numbers on the side of a reform produces a psychological influence which acts upon the minds of rulers, and so soon as Socialism becomes popular, or even before then, when it is recognised by thinkers that Socialism offers the one chance left of saving our civilisation from being destroyed by wealth and poverty, great statesmen and philosophers will arise and take their stand boldly with the people in their fight for industrial freedom. Wycliffe, John Ball, Gerrard Winstanley, Sir Thomas More, Robert Owen, Ernest Jones, Charles Kingsley, Frederic Denison Maurice, Frederic Harrison, Cardinal Manning, and William Morris, are among the names which occur to me as being of the type I have in my mind. The workers of Greece had their Solon, of Sparta their Lycurgus, of

Italy their Spartacus, of Germany their Huss in the hour of their social need, and the mould from which these Social Giants was formed cannot have been altogether destroyed.

In Great Britain two sets of influences are at work bringing the more intellectually minded of the middle-class over to Socialism. There is the increasing tension required in the conduct of business which so saps a man's energies as to leave him little of either time or inclination for the cultivation of any other than the business faculty. A tendency to revolt against this is a well-marked feature of the social life of our time. Of what use is it, ask these slaves of the ledger, to spend the greater part of a lifetime in acquiring a competency only to find after it has been acquired that its acquisition has taken all the savour of enjoyment out of life? It is surprising the charm which Socialism has for men and women of this type. Others come to Socialism through intellectual conviction and humanitarian promptings. The terrible lot of the people, from which there is no way of escape, harries their feelings and overrides all consideration of their own selfish material interests. Kinship with their fellows is more to them than their rent-rolls or their scrip, and these too, in gradually increasing numbers, are boldly championing the Socialist cause. When the Socialist propaganda takes more cognisance of this class and makes special efforts to reach them, especially in their school or college days, a rich harvest of results will be reaped.

But it is to the working-class itself that we must look for changing the system of production and making it a means of providing for the healthy human need of all the people. This is so not only because of their numbers but also because unless they consciously set themselves to win Socialism it can never be won. It is, in the fullest sense of a very much abused phrase, a People's Cause. When it has been won it will be their fight which has won it; should it never be won, and should our Western civilisation totter on until it falls into the depths of a merciful oblivion, that too will be their doing, and be due entirely to their not having had the courage and the intelligence to put up a fight strong enough to save it and themselves.

Hitherto the workers have been content to ask for small reforms; now they are realising that private property is the enemy they have to encounter. The property question is the issue which is creating a new political cleavage in the State. Somewhat dimly at present, but with growing clearness of vision, the worker begins to see that he will remain a menial, outcast and forlorn, until he has made himself master of the machine he tends and the soil he tills. Hence the growth of Socialism.

What indications, then, are there that the working-class are likely to prove equal to the occasion, and play the heroic part which is theirs in the evolution of a juster state of society? I deem the signs many and great. Once again the instinct of the worker has proved itself a surer guide than the philosophies of the Schoolmen. At a time when Individualism, imported from France by the way, was taking firm hold over the minds of Radical economists and philosophers in Great Britain, the workmen were flying directly in the teeth of all that was being preached to them. Individualism meant, *inter alia,* the absolute freedom of a man to sell his labour in the way which his own individual interests might decide him to deem the best, and anything which in any way interfered with this freedom of action on his part was, he was assured by the wise men, a thing accursed. Further, he was assured, that any interference with the free play of capital would bring heavy punishment in its train. All

the time that this was being proclaimed to
the workman, he, in the face of public opinion
and of legal enactment, was sturdily building up his trade-union organisation, the
primary object of which was to restrain
individual action, and put a curb upon capital when it sought to impose too harsh conditions upon his labour. For nearly three
quarters of a century the unequal struggle
for the legal recognition of Trade Unions and
the right to combine was kept up between the
voteless workman on the one side and the
forces of law, savagely administered, and
public opinion on the other. The workman
won, although not until he had been enfranchised in the big towns.

There are now two and a quarter million
trade-union workers organised for mutual aid
and support, and a feeling of solidarity is
growing inside the movement which is full
of promise. Just as the small business is
being swallowed up in the big Combine, so
are the separate Unions drawing together
into Federations, and these in turn are uniting into one all-embracing Federation. The
great Co-operative movement and the Friendly
Orders for succour in sickness and old age, are
further evidences of the instinct of the working-
class for combined action. It may be alleged,

and with some truth, that no great Altruistic ideal underlies any of these movements, and that at most they are merely forms of insurance against eventualities. That, however, is beside the point. The fact which I am seeking to illustrate is that the working-class is developing a sense of solidarity, of standing by each other, and of sinking self in what is meant to be the good of all. A people which has got thus far will be prepared to go a good deal further as its outlook broadens, its understanding deepens, and as the occasion demands. The greatest sign of hope of all, however, is the evolution of a political Labour Party. Here also the intuition of the worker is carrying him away from the tutelage of his would-be mentors. In at least thirty constituencies at the General Election of 1906 his vote returned Labour men to Parliament, many of them avowed Socialists, and all of them independent. In almost as many more constituencies similar candidates only just failed of being successful. The evidence which this fact affords of the growing faith of the worker in himself and of his determination to hew a pathway through the briar entanglement in which he finds himself is self-evident. Thus on every side we are made aware of the growing consciousness of the working-class movement

C

and of the earnestness by which it is characterised. Already it is largely a Socialist movement, and is in continual process of becoming more so. With the speculative side of Socialism the average man with us has but small concern; it is its common sense which appeals to him. By inherited instinct we are all Communists at heart; and if the isolated Ego of self gets the upper hand for a time he produces results so terrifying that the mistake of allowing him to rule is speedily made apparent, and we begin to seek a way whereby we may return to the kindly sway of the spirit of Altruism. For a full rounded century the gospel of Selfishness has held sway, and under it the nation has stumbled on from one depth to another until it has reached the verge of a precipice from the void of which there can be no re-ascent should we be dragged over. Poverty, physical deterioration, insanity, are evils which no nation can suffer and yet live. They are all three the direct product of the competitive system of wealth production; and it is, or should be, the first and most urgent business of the State to uproot the upas tree which bears such deadly fruit.

CHAPTER IV

SOCIALISM AND CHRISTIANITY

SOCIALISM, like every other problem of life, is at bottom a question of ethics or morals. It has mainly to do with the relationships which should exist between a man and his fellows. Civilisation, even in its lowest forms, necessitates that people should live together as an organism since only thus is life with any degree of security and of intellectual companionship possible. As Kropotkin has shown, the weakest and most inoffensive of the lower animals are able to hold their own against the strongest and most ferocious by congregating together in societies. Since, then, community of life in one form or another is inevitable, Socialism challenges that conception of Society which regards each unit as being at war with every other and which raises artificial barriers between individuals and classes, and thus hinders that free intercourse and community of feeling and interest which is so necessary to the promotion of happiness. If under the present system the poor are made prisoners by their poverty, the rich are made no less so by their wealth. Every relationship in life is vitiated by the false basis upon which Society rests.

The charge that Socialism is a materialistic creed comes with a bad grace from those whose every waking hour is spent either in striving to accumulate wealth at the expense of their neighbours, or in sensuous and luxurious enjoyment of the pleasures of life. It cannot be too emphatically stated that Socialism takes no more cognisance of the religious opinions of its adherents than does either Liberalism or Conservatism. It would, however, be an easy task to show that Communism, the final goal of Socialism, is a form of Social Economy very closely akin to the principles set forth in the Sermon on the Mount. Christ recognised clearly that the possession of private property came between a man and his welfare both for time and eternity; and every great religious and moral teacher whom the world has ever known has denounced wealth and eulogised poverty. They have done so, not in the sense that poverty, meaning the absence of the necessaries and conveniences of life, is a thing either good or desirable in itself, but to emphasise the fact that riches and property are things inherently evil when personally owned and possessed. We have but to listen to a sermon in any church in Christendom to learn how far this interpretation of Christianity is opposed to modern religious opinion, and yet I hold it to be the doctrine upon which Christianity and Socialism are alike based. The Mosaic laws for the regulation of the holding of land and the treatment of the poor and the unfortunate cannot perhaps be described as Socialistic in the modern sense of the word. When we remember, however, that they were framed to meet the needs of a people just emerging from the nomadic pastoral state, in which Communism of a crude but effective sort had been practised, and were intended to put a check upon the growing rapacity of those early Individualists who were adding field to field and plying the usurer's calling, we see that they were quite as drastic in their way as are many of the Socialist proposals of our day. Usury was prohibited, land could neither be sold outright nor held for more than a limited period as security for debt ; even the debtor was freed from all obligations when the year of jubilee came round. The prophets and preachers of the pre-Christian era were loud in their denunciations of the folly of those who expected happiness from riches. They beheld the tears of the oppressed, and saw that on the side of the oppressors there was wealth and power. They declared that the profit of the earth was for all, and that even the king was dependent upon the field for his daily food. Men were heaping up riches which they could not enjoy and were only thereby adding to their own hurt, labouring for the wind. Social equality and fierce denunciations of the rich form the staple of the writings we are now taught to look upon as having been inspired. As Renan has it: The prophets of Israel are fiery publicists of the description we should now call Socialists or Anarchists. They are fanatical in their demands for social justice, and proclaim aloud that, if the world is not just nor capable of becoming just, it were better it were destroyed. The rich man was an impious extortioner, whilst he who deprived the workman of his wages was stigmatised as a murderer. Clearly the modern system of wealth accumulation, which is rooted and grounded in land monopoly, usury, and the fleecing of the poor, finds no support in such teachings as are contained in the Old Testament Scriptures.

The Sermon on the Mount, whilst it perhaps lends but small countenance to State Socialism, is full of the spirit of pure Communism. Nay, in its lofty contempt for thrift and forethought, it goes far in advance of anything ever put forward by any Communist, ancient or modern. Christ's denunciations of wealth are only equalled by the fierceness of the diatribes which He levelled against the Pharisees. It was St. Paul who enunciated the doctrine that he who would not work neither should he eat, whilst St. James in his Epistle rivals the old prophets in his treatment of those who grow rich at the expense of the poor. Contrary to the generally accepted opinion, it is now known that Communism in goods was practised by Christians for at least three hundred years after the death of Christ. Almost without exception, the early Christian Fathers whose teachings have come down to us spoke out fearlessly against usury, which includes interest also, and on the side of Communism. They proclaimed that, inasmuch as nature had provided all things in common, it was sinful robbery for one man to own more than another, especially if that other was in want. The man who gathered much whilst others had not enough, was a murderer. The poor had a right to their share of everything there was, which is different from the charity so common nowadays. If a man inherited wealth he was, if not a robber himself, but the recipient of stolen goods, since no accumulation of wealth could be come by honestly. To those who said that the idleness of the poor was the cause of their poverty, St. John Chrysostom replied that the rich too were idlers living on their plunder.

For seven hundred years, says one authority, almost all the Fathers of the Church considered Communism the most perfect and most Christian form of Social organisation, and it was only after Christianity, from being the despised and persecuted creed of the poor, had become the official religion of the State, that opinion on this point began to undergo a change. Even then it was not until the thirteenth century that the Church came out into the open as a defender of property. All the great semi-religious semi-political movements from the twelfth to the seventeenth century, had a Communistic basis. In fact, there is good reason to believe that they had their origin in the teachings of the Weaving Friars, a semi-religious and strongly Communistic Trade Guild formed in Bruges by the Flemish woollen weavers towards the end of the twelfth century. Whether this was so or not, this at least is not open to dispute, that the Peasant Revolt in England—led by John Ball, "the Mad Priest of Kent"—drew its inspiration from the Communistic teachings of Wycliffe; that when, ten years later, Bohemia was in revolt, the leader was John Huss the Communist; when in 1525 (April 2nd) the Peasants' War broke out simultaneously all over Germany, Saxony, and Switzerland, it was the teachings of Thomas Munster, the German Communist, which were, and rightly, credited with being the cause. The world-famous Anabaptist movement which followed was avowedly Communistic. All of these risings met with a common fate; Church and State combined their forces and suppressed them with even more than the usual savage barbarity and inhuman cruelty of the age.

During the Commonwealth period in England some 5000 of Cromwell's Roundheads tried to induce the Protector to adopt a Socialist constitution for the Commonwealth. We have Cromwell's own authority for saying that Lilburne's Levellers, as they were contemptuously nicknamed, wanted " to make the tenant as liberal a fortune as the landlord." Such rank heresy to the Commonwealth had of course to be stamped out at all costs, and Cromwell put as much energy into the work of putting down the Communists of his own ranks—though they had fought with him and for him—as he did into that for the suppression of the rebellious Irish kernes. In fact, some of the shootings which took place read almost like scenes from the horrors which accompanied the suppression of the Commune of Paris in 1871. All this, it may truly be said, is no evidence that Communism is the best form of Government, but it is evidence so strong as to be irrefutable that Christianity in its pristine purity had Communism as its invariable outcome, and that for nearly seventeen centuries the common people and their leaders believed Communism and Christianity to be synonymous terms. Incidentally it shows how little modern church-goers know of the history of their own religion when they charge Socialism with being anti-Christian.

Socialists, in common with the early Christian fathers, recognise, that it is futile to proclaim fraternity and community of interest unless they at the same time provide the environment and conditions of life which make these possible. It is a mockery to proclaim a high ideal to people whilst supporting a system which makes it impossible for the ideal ever to be realised. Let me illustrate this by a simple illustration. It is estimated that there are 120,000 women in the metropolis alone living on the earnings of shame. Suppose some great preacher, some modern Savonarola, to enter upon a crusade amongst these women, and to succeed in awakening within them—no difficult task by

the way—a desire to leave the life they now lead
and to enter upon one of honest work, where in
all the land are 120,000 situations to be found
to which they may turn ?   If those good folks
who preach the higher life, leaving all worldly
considerations out of account, will but master
this simple elementary fact, many of the problems which now to them appear insoluble will
have been solved.   Men do not gather grapes
from thorns, nor figs from thistles, and it is for
this reason that Socialists concentrate their
efforts upon a change of the system under which
wealth is produced—and which enables the
strong and the unscrupulous to prey upon
the community and condemns the mass of the
people to a life of toil and poverty—as an indispensable preliminary to that further development of the higher forms of life which they, in
common with all reformers, desire to see.   To
the taunt that this is beginning at the wrong
end, the obvious retort is that the other method
has been tried for centuries with what results
we know only too well.   It is not without
significance that many of the best known
present-day leaders of religious thought are
avowed Socialists in the modern sense of
the word, and if they claim the right to call
themselves Christian Socialists, no one who
knows anything of the history of Christianity

will challenge their right to use the prefix. My purpose in writing this chapter will have been served if I have succeeded in showing that the Socialist who denounces rent and interest as robbery, and who seeks the abolition of the system which legalises such, is in the true line of apostolic succession with the pre-Christian era prophets, with the Divine Founder of Christianity, and with those who for the first seven hundred years of the Christian faith maintained even to the death the unsullied right of their religious faith to be regarded as the Gospel of the poor. Surely if Socialism can enable man

> To stand from fear set free, to breathe and wait,
> To hold a hand uplifted over Hate,

it will be, if not a religion in itself, at least a handmaiden to religion, and as such entitled to the support of all who pray for the coming of Christ's Kingdom upon earth. For—

> Methinks, if nought be done to ease the pain,
> The weariness, the hunger, and the fret
> Of life on earth, there is no hope in heaven
> For the dumb workers with dull crowded brain
> And tired bodies that crave nought but sleep.

CHAPTER V

SOCIALISM AND THE WORKER

ACCORDING to Professor Thorold Rogers the golden age of the English workman was the fifteenth century. Food was cheap, wages high, and an eight-hour day the rule. An artisan who boarded out had to pay from ninepence to one shilling per week for food and lodging, whilst his wages ranged from three shillings to four shillings per week of forty-eight hours. In 1495, according to the same authority, an artisan could provision his family for a whole year out of the earnings of ten weeks' work, whilst an agricultural labourer could do the same with fifteen weeks' work. It appears to have been common in those far-off days to pay for Sundays and holidays when there was no work done. Nor was this state of things peculiar to England. It is now known that a similar state of things obtained in France and Saxony. In the latter place we are told a stone mason in the fifteenth century could buy with his week's wages three sheep and one pair of shoes. There were in addition to Sundays thirty-four holidays or Church festivals in the course of the year—eighty-six days in all on which no work was done, and in addition work ceased at four o'clock on Saturdays and on twenty-five other Fair days. Rogers particularly mentions the fifteenth and the first quarter of the sixteenth century as limiting the duration of this golden age. More recent investigations, however, have confirmed his guess that, taking Europe as a whole, it lasted from the beginning of the thirteenth to the middle of the fifteenth century, or roughly from two hundred to three hundred years, and there were neither Millionaires nor Paupers in those days, but a rude abundance for all. Two main causes seem to have been at work in producing it: the rising of the peasants in the country districts, and the growth of towns, with the free communal life which characterised them and the enormous areas of the Common lands. In addition, the Plague or Black Death and the wars of the period had thinned the population, and in the towns each trade was strongly protected by its Guild. Whatever these may have developed into in their later stages, they were originally the equivalent of our modern Trade Unions. It is interesting to note that we have records of these Unions as far back as history carries. Greece in its palmiest days knew their strength, as did also Rome when in the heyday of its power. The resurrected inscriptions on the walls of buried Pompeii include a nomination by the members of the Fishermen's Union of one of their number to a seat on the Board of Works, and of "Mrs. Cappella" to act as a magistrate. Direct Labour Representation and Women Suffrage are thus shown to have quite a respectable antiquity to recommend them.

In England it took the State two hundred years to reduce the worker, town and country alike, from independent affluence to a poverty-stricken condition. Legislation for regulating wages and for chaining the worker to one parish, to fix the kind of cloth he should dress in, the number of hours he should work, and other like regulations intended to weaken the power of the working-class, had all been tried; but it was only when the land was taken from the peasants, the commons confiscated, and the Guilds broken up, and, finally, when the price of food had been doubled and quadrupled through the operations of a debased coinage, that success attended these maleficent acts. The Protestant Reformation, by despoiling the monasteries of their lands, the one refuge to which the needy worker could fly for succour, also told heavily against the poor, whilst the new gospel of individual salvation lent the sanction of religion to the selfish creed of each for himself which was then just beginning to assert itself as the dominant principle in business. Under its baneful influence old customs and habits and the old communal traditional life of the people in town and country were ruthlessly broken and destroyed, and that era of desolation and barren inhumanity entered upon from which we are now only just beginning to emerge. For, as I show in another chapter, the prosperity of the worker was coincident with, and its continuance in no small measure attributable to, a period chiefly remarkable for the strong element of Communism which characterised town and village life. If the Anabaptists and the various other sects who had sought to make Communism and Christianity synonymous terms had been washed out in a tempest of blood and flame, much of their spirit remained. It was not for nothing that John Ball and Wat Tyler had taught the peasantry of England the doctrine of the dignity of manhood and the emptiness of titles.

John Stuart Mill expressed a doubt whether all the mechanical inventions of the nineteenth century had lightened the labour of one human being. The social investigator of the twentieth century is prepared to affirm positively that the lot of the poor in normal times under Capitalism is worse than it ever could have been in normal times in any previous period in British history. Production, say the Fawcetts in their lectures on Social and Political subjects, has been stimulated beyond the expectations of the most sanguine; still, however, so far as the labourer is concerned, the age of golden plenty seems as remote as ever, and in the humble homes of the poor a no less constant war has to be waged against penury and want. This, however, is but half the truth. The conditions attendant upon poverty in these latter days are more demoralising than ever before. In the less complex life of former days the poor were more akin to other classes, and better able to help themselves. In the great vortex of modern life they are almost completely shut off from human fellowship. The stress and strain are so great, the organisation of Society so anarchic, that once a man gets down into the depths his chances of rising again are exceedingly remote.

I know that it is a commonplace of the Jeremiahs of every age to hold that the men of former ages were better than those of their own. In certain respects I confess that I rank with those who believe that we have deteriorated,

D

especially in the sphere of intellect, since the days of our great-grandparents. The stage, the press, and the pulpit could easily be cited as evidence in support of this. The plays of Shakespeare were performed, even in his own day, to crowded audiences without the scenic effects and curtailment which are now necessary to make them acceptable to the modern play-goer. Any one familiar with the popular litera-ture of the Radical and Chartist movements of the opening and middle years of last century will see how far its modern successor falls below the standard of those days. The solid sermon and newspaper articles of even half-a-hundred years ago would not now be tolerated; not because of their dulness, but because of the mental effort needed to follow and understand them. A snippety press and a sensational pulpit are outstanding marks of modern times. Nor are the reasons far to seek. Previous to the introduction of machinery and the factory system every workman was an individual. They were not herded together in masses, regimented, numbered, and specialised. The blacksmith, the weaver, the carpenter, the shoemaker, and the tailor either worked direct for their own customers or for masters only a very small degree removed from them-selves. A master was in those days more of a master workman than an employer. Each journeyman could confidently look forward to the time when he too would be a master. The master's income rarely exceeded by more than 20 per cent. the wage of his workmen, with whom he freely mingled both in work and play. It was only when machinery and the factory system were introduced that great fortunes began to be accumulated and masters and workmen separated into distinct classes with an ever-widening breach between them. When working for themselves, as a very large proportion of the old-time craftsmen did, they started work in the morning when it pleased them, broke off during the day as it suited them, and left off in the evening according to the necessities of the moment or their own whim or convenience. Each such man was his own master; he owned the tools wherewith he worked, and the product was his own property when completed. A man had some pride in the labour of his hands, some incentive to do his best, since his good name was at stake in every job he turned out. Under those conditions the tendency was to develop individuality. The free exchange of opinion which resulted from men of this type meeting together for a social glass or pipe developed an intellectuality which we look for in vain in the modern factory hand.

Nor is this all. The uncertainty and irresponsibility of the modern workman's lot in life must produce evil effects upon his character.

We are all more or less the products of our environment, and modern workshop conditions are not conducive to the production of either intellect or individuality. The workman is called into the workshop when capital can profitably employ him, and turned adrift again the moment capital finds it can no longer turn his services to profitable account. He is not consulted as to when he shall be employed or when cast adrift. His necessities and those of his dependants are no concern of any one save himself. He has no right to employment, no one is under obligation to find him work, nor is he free to work for himself since he has neither the use of land nor the command of the necessary capital. He must be more or less of a nomad, ready to go at a moment's notice to where a job is vacant. He may be starving, but may not grow food ; naked, but may not weave cloth ; homeless, but may not build a house. When in work he has little if any say in the regulations which govern the factory, and none in deciding what work is to be done or how it is to be done. His duty begins and ends in doing as he is bid. To talk to a neighbour workman at the bench is an offence punishable by a fine ; so, too, in some cases is whistling while at work. At a given hour in the morning the factory bell warns him that it is time to be inside the gate ready for the machines to start ; at a set hour the bell or hooter calls him out to dinner and again recalls him to his task one hour later. He does not own the machines he manipulates, nor does he own the product of his labour. He is a hireling, and glad to be any man's hireling who will find him work. During one period when trade is good he is not only fully employed but has to work overtime ; at another when trade is slack he is only partially employed, if employed at all. The result of all this is to produce demoralisation of the most fatal kind. There is no sense of unity between the man and his work. He can have no pride in it since there is nothing personal to him which will attach to it after it is finished. It will be sold he knows not by whom nor to whom. All day long he works under the eye of a taskmaster set over him to see that he does not shirk his duties. At the end of the week he is paid so many shillings for what he has done, and, naturally enough, his one concern is with the number of shillings he will receive. This is the cash nexus which binds him to his employer, who, by the way, is very likely a huge impersonal soulless concern known as a company. Of the individuals composing it he knows nothing, nor they of him.

There is no sense of honour or of Chivalry in business. A big wealthy concern will cheat its workpeople of their wages, or spend thousands in resisting the claim to compensation of some poor widow or orphan whose husband or father has been killed in their service. It is not that employers are inhuman ; but their connection with their workpeople is a business one, from which every trace of human feeling has been carefully excluded.

> Time has no birthday gifts for such as these,
> A human herd of starved and stunted growth,
> That knows not how to walk, to whom the speech
> Of England, of the land that gave them birth,
> Comes twisted, harsh and scarce articulate,
> Whose minds lie fallow, while they chew the cud
> Of hunger, darkness, impotence, disease.

As old age approaches—and for the workman this may mean anything over forty—a cold grey terror begins to take possession of his heart. Fight against it as he may, he cannot get away from the fact that within the circle of his acquaintance there are men just turned forty, as good workmen as himself, for whom the ordinary labour market no longer has any use. He knows his turn will also come some day. A slackness of trade, some petty offence which in a younger man would pass unnoticed, and out he goes to return no more. Then begins life's tragedy in grim earnest. From place to place he goes in search of a job. He knows himself to be still capable of much good work. To the business man forty-five is the period of life at which he is at his best; it is also the age at which a rising statesman enters upon his career, when the powers of the artist and the man of letters are at their fullest. But all this only adds bitterness to the cup of humiliation which the aged workman has now to drain to the dregs. Most large establishments have a standing order that no one over forty-five is to be given employment; with many the age limit is forty; whilst in one case to which publicity was recently given it is as low as thirty-five. And so the aged workman who has too much honour left to lie about his age and too much honesty to use hair dye, at last wearies of his vain quest for what will never again be his, a steady job at his own trade, and resorts to any odd job which turns up. As for savings to meet a case of this kind, that is usually quite out of the question. The thrifty, steady workman who is a member of a trade union and a benefit society is entitled to certain old age benefits, but these do not accrue until he is fifty-five or sixty; and although it is common to stretch the rules of these organisations to meet the more deserving cases, obviously the funds would not stand the strain of meeting all of them. Besides, not more than one half of the working people are in a position to make any such provision for old age. The earnings of the working-class only average about 21s. 6d. a week. That figure, be it remembered, is got by taking the total income of all who are not paid more than £160 a year and dividing it by the number of wage-workers. But low as this figure must appear to the comfortable classes, it does not reveal the whole truth. Knowing the facts both from personal experience and a thorough familiarity with the circumstances, I assert fearlessly that one half of the adult workers of Great Britain earn less than one pound per week, year in and year out, when in work. This leaves no margin for saving, nor does it provide even that subsistence wage which the economists are so fond of telling us competition will not fail to provide for the worker. Perhaps this can best be brought out by a reference to a work the conclusions of which have never been seriously challenged. In his painstaking

and exhaustive inquiry into the condition of
the people of York, a typical industrial town,
Mr. Seebohm Rowntree arrived at pretty
much the same conclusion as was reached by
Mr. Charles Booth when he made a similar
inquiry concerning the life of the people of
London.   Mr. Rowntree says that in York the
minimum upon which bare physical efficiency
can be maintained is 21s. 8d. a week, and that
in a year of abounding trade and prosperity he
found that forty-five per cent. of the working-
class, taking their income from every source
and treating the family earning as a unit for
the purpose of the calculation, were receiving
less than this sum, and consequently were in
poverty.   Here is his definition of poverty:—

It is thus seen that *the wages paid for unskilled
labour in York are insufficient to provide food, shelter,
and clothing adequate to maintain a family of moderate size in a state of bare physical efficiency.*   It will
be remembered that the above estimates of necessary minimun expenditure are based upon the assumption that the diet is even less generous than
that allowed to able-bodied paupers in the York
Workhouse, and that *no allowance is made for any
expenditure other than that absolutely required for
the maintenance of merely physical efficiency.*

And let us clearly understand what "merely
physical efficiency" means.   A family living upon

the scale allowed for in this estimate must never spend a penny on railway fare or omnibus. They must never go into the country unless they walk. They must never purchase a halfpenny newspaper or spend a penny to buy a ticket for a popular concert. They must write no letters to absent children, for they cannot afford to pay the postage. They must never contribute anything to their church or chapel, or give any help to a neighbour which costs them money. They cannot save, nor can they join sick club or trade union, because they cannot pay the necessary subscriptions. The children must have no pocket money for dolls, marbles, or sweets. The father must smoke no tobacco, and must drink no beer. The mother must never buy any pretty clothes for herself or for her children, the character of the family wardrobe as for the family diet being governed by the regulation, Nothing must be bought but that which is absolutely necessary for the maintenance of physical health, and what is bought must be of the plainest and most economical description. Should a child fall ill, it must be attended by the parish doctor; should it die it must be buried by the parish. Finally the wage-earner must never be absent from his work for a single day.

If any of these conditions are broken, the extra expenditure is met, *and can only be met*, by limiting the diet, or, in other words, by sacrificing physical efficiency. . . . It cannot, therefore, be too clearly understood, nor too emphatically repeated, *that whenever a worker having three children dependent on him, and receiving not more than 21s. per week, indulges in any expenditure beyond that required for the barest physical needs, he can do so only at the cost of his own physical efficiency, or of that of some members of his family.*

The italics are the author's. These, then, are the causes which have led to the intellectual and moral deterioration of the working-class. Under all these circumstances the workmen would have been different from every other created being had he not deteriorated physically and mentally. True, we have got over the worst in this respect, and already a very decided change is noticeable among the younger men. From 1780 to 1850 was a transition period, and then the process of demoralisation was doing its worst. The generation following inherited all the bad effects of the conditions which had been prevailing, but the young generation of to-day, thoroughly in touch with their environment and intelligently conscious of the causes which make them the slaves of the machine, are in full revolt; and just as the awakened serfs of the thirteenth century carved their way to comparative freedom and prosperity, so too shall the awakening proletariat of the twentieth century. But the foundation on which they shall build their industrial freedom shall be more abiding than any which has gone before. When the modern industrial movement reaches fruition, land, capital, and the State itself shall all be owned and controlled by the useful classes. There shall be no longer an exploiting class left to reduce the workers again to penury and want by the methods which, as we have seen, were so successful in the Middle Ages. Socialism, by taking away the power to exploit, ensures permanent freedom for all.

CHAPTER VI

SOCIALISM AND THE WOMAN QUESTION

IN a state of Society in which strength and brutality are the ruling factors, the gentle and weak must go to the wall. At a very early stage, therefore, in the evolution of the race woman must have come under the subjection of man. It is a great defect to be weak, says Letourneau, even in our most civilised societies, but in the early stage of human development it is an unpardonable wrong. Woman's recurring periods of maternity, and the love for her offspring which grew out of it, must, apart from other reasons, have handicapped her seriously, especially during the nomadic period. Be the cause what it may, we know that amongst savage races the woman is the drudge, the beast of burden who does all the hard and disagreeable work, whilst her lord and master hunts and fishes, or smokes and basks in the sun. She is, in these cases, treated as a rule as being on the same level with the slaves. She has no rights, and may be maltreated or killed by her paramour without let or hindrance. Curiously enough, women seem to have been the first form of private property. She it was who first "belonged" to some man. After a time, when the family became more or less of an institution, it was through the mother that property descended, a form, by the way, which seems to have survived until quite a recent period amongst Celtic peoples. The mythical lore of most nations, especially the Celts, frequently shows the woman as the hero, which may however be simply, like so many other things in mythology, a reminiscence from some golden age of humanity which has completely vanished from our ken. Be that as it may, so far as history shows, woman has all down through the ages been the burden-bearer. Occasionally we get glimpses of what appears to be a new era dawning for women, as when Mrs. Cappella is being nominated for election to the Board of Education in Pompeii; but a little more investigation reveals the fact that these favoured women of antiquity were frequently the courtesans and not the douce mothers of families. The position of the courtesan in the ancient empires of the East has never been fully explained. It is certain, however, that she occupied a place of honour and was accorded rights, liberties, and privileges which were jealously withheld from her virtuous sister. May I suggest that her economic independence probably affords a key to the explanation ? It is the absence of this which, whether in man or woman, leads to their captivity by others on whom they have to depend for a livelihood, and the married woman is nearly always, unfortunately, a dependent. Even in those instances where she is not, the force of habit produces in her the same attitude of mind and will as is shown by those who are.

The position of women would, I submit, be revolutionised by Socialism. The Sex problem is at bottom the Labour problem. All questions of women's rights and wrongs, including the marriage laws, resolve themselves in their final analysis into this—that she is economically dependent upon man. In the sphere of industry woman is beginning to take an ever-increasing part, and in many cases is being used as a weapon wherewith to beat down the wages of men. In one or two instances, especially in the textile industries, where the trade union organisation is strong, women receive equal rates of pay when doing the same work as men, but this is the exception. In the East End of London, and, in fact, in the east of every great city,

there is a class of women workers whose
condition is too pitiable for language to describe. They occupy the lowest place of any
in the industrial scale, and seem, at present,
the most helpless and consequently the most
hopeless portion of the community. I was
not, however, thinking of the sweated industrial woman only when I spoke of economic
dependence. The daughter of the middle-
class man, trained to play the fine lady, is
usually dependent upon a successful marriage
for the means of keeping up her position. In
the ranks of the working-class the same thing
applies. The average young woman of the
working-class, who is not herself employed
in some well-paid occupation, has nothing but
marriage to which to look forward. She gives
herself and all she has or is in exchange for
such board as her husband's means permit.
So long as the present system of wealth production and distribution continues, it is difficult
to say how this could be changed. In ancient
Rome, under Augustus, the law *Julia et Papia
Poppœa* compelled a wealthy father to give his
marriageable daughter a substantial dowry.
Even were this revived, it could only benefit a
privileged few. Recently, proposals have been
seriously put forward for the endowment of
Motherhood by the State. This, however, has

been more in connection with a desire to prevent the race suicide which is threatened by the way in which the families of the well-to-do and more intelligent members of the community are being limited to two or three children, than from any real desire to improve the mother's position as a woman. The old-fashioned type of woman is becoming scarce. She was not only willing to bear a large family, but in addition to play a part in the domestic economy of the nation the value of which has not, I think, been sufficiently appreciated. The type of woman whom I have in my mind was she, who, in addition to being a wife and the mother of eight or ten children, also undertook the duties of house-keeper, cook, tablemaid, nurse, charwoman, washerwoman, laundrymaid, and general slavey in a house of one or two rooms, on a wage of from 20s. to 30s. a week—often on less. The best of these working wives and mothers are the most remarkable instances on record of patient uncomplaining industry and inherited skill. For not only did they get through their work, but they performed each and every one of their multifarious tasks as though it had been their one and only occupation. Oh the pathos of those bright, clean, bien, couthie cottage homes, with the thrifty mother never

E

idle, and never fussed, patching, darning, knitting or sewing, keeping the cradle gently rocking with a light touch of her foot as she crooned some old ballad or soothing lullaby to keep her last born quiet, whilst she plied her needle and shears ! She ruled her little kingdom in love and gentle firmness, often, I fear, without that appreciation which was her due. She was a National Asset of priceless worth. But these too are going out, as the handicraftsmen have gone, and their place soon shall know them no more, and the world is growing a colder and poorer place for lack of them. Capitalism has much to answer for.

The modern woman is of quite a different type. She prefers the comparative freedom of the factory or the shop or office, to the eternal drudgery and espionage of domestic service. When married she gets from the market many of the wares which her forebear made with her own hands. Knitting and sewing are not to her taste, and she considers herself disgraced if her family exceeds two or three children. She is infected by the restless spirit of the age, and is no longer the contented domestic drudge so common a generation or so ago. She is clamouring for the vote, and will ere long succeed in winning it. Whether it will realise all she expects from it when it has been won is more than doubtful, but at least it will place her on terms of political equality with man.

Now I regard all this, with all its drawbacks, as a healthy sign of the times—as an indication, in fact, of better times in store for mankind. Unrest and discontent are the heralds of coming change, the forerunners of reform. The more women agitate, the deeper they probe into their grievances, the more clearly will it be borne in upon them that the real root cause of all their trouble is their economic dependence upon man. Under Socialism when the woman, whether as wife, mother or worker, will, have a claim in her own right to a share in the national wealth, she will at once emerge into greater freedom. In choosing a mate she will no longer be driven by hard economic necessity to accept the most eligible offer from the worldly point of view, but will be guided exclusively by all-compelling love and the need for congenial companionship. Biologists tell us that it is to natural selection we owe the development and improvement of the species. The strong, good-looking male attracts the best of the females, and thus the best qualities on both sides get transmitted to offspring and are by them passed on to succeeding generations until they become permanently incorporated. This is the real struggle there is in the animal kingdom, the struggle of the best for partnership with the best. Dr. Karl Pearson, and other authorities, have been warning us that the unfit and the less fit are multiplying in Great Britain at a rate out of all proportion to the more fit, and that in this direction also we are making at headlong pace for race suicide. This too is purely a question of economics. The very poor have no sense of responsibility, and give a looser rein to the passions than their better fed, housed, clothed, conditioned and, consequently, better controlled neighbours. I think too it may be found to be a biological fact that a badly nutritioned, and consequently ill-conditioned loose organism is more prolific than one more firmly knit; and also that as intellect grows the reproductive organs become less fruitful. Be that as it may, one thing is certain : were women freed from their economic bondage to man, they would have a freer choice than at present in the selection of a father for their children, and the tendency would then be for the less fit to get left and the more fit taken, and, as a consequence, and without any outside interference, such as is sometimes suggested, the race would begin to improve straight away.

For woman, as for man therefore, it is to Socialism we must look. No reform of the marriage law, or of the franchise laws, will of themselves materially alter her condition. At best the vote is but a means to an end, and the end is freedom, and freedom means the right to live and to the means of life in exchange for the performance of some duty to the community. The time will come when motherhood will be regarded as the most sacred of all duties, and will be rewarded accordingly.

Socialism means, then, that the sexes shall meet on terms of freedom and equality. How else can we hope for real progress? If there is a taint of dependence anywhere it pollutes the whole of life's atmosphere. It may be that there are, as is said, physiological differences which make it impossible for men and women ever to be physically equal. But if there be one glory of the sun and another of the moon they are each equal within their own domain, and it is only by a recognition of this law of equality that a material universe is possible at all. In like manner it is only by recognising the perfect right of every human being to equal treatment because they are human beings that we can hope for better days for the race, and it is only when humanity, weary of the burden which Materialism has placed upon its bent and drooping shoulders, resolves to stand erect in the truth of a perfect equality, that it can hope to be saved from its self-imposed sorrow and suffering.

CHAPTER VII

FROM SERFDOM TO SOCIALISM

THE modern Socialist movement is but a continuation of the fight for freedom which the disinherited have been waging since long ere yet history carries any record of man's doings. Sociology—a science still in its infancy—leaves us in no doubt as to the process by which the mass of the people have been brought under subjection to the few. A nomadic herd of only partially developed human beings barely one degree removed from the brute and in which the family tie has not yet emerged, finally settles on some favoured spot. In process of time it becomes a settled community, owning all things in common, and living mainly by the produce of the chase. As experience develops intelligence, crude forms of agriculture begin to make their appearance; certain animals are domesticated, and the family tie is slowly evolved. Property, hitherto confined to weapons of the chase, usually buried with their owner, expands until it includes the produce of some particular bit of soil, and inheritance follows in the wake of its growth. By this time the undisciplined horde has evolved some settled form of government, and is in a fair way to becoming prosperous. In the main it remains Communistic save in the matter of personal belongings, which may now include cattle. About this period, however, one of two things, sometimes both, usually happen which gradually changes the entire outlook for the little village commonwealth. Either a ruling caste is set up which acquires more and more control over the land from which all alike draw their sustenance until it finally succeeds in reducing the mass of the people to a condition of dependence upon its will, or some other and stronger tribe, regarding its neighbour's goods with covetous eye, invades and subdues and conquers the community, and reduces it to a state of bondage to its conquerors. For the sake of clearness I have reduced the process to its simplest form, and the reader has but to expand the illustration until the nation takes the place of the settlement to have a picture presented to his mind's eye of how in the earlier stages of progress man is brought into subjection to his fellow. Private property and war have been the great enslavers since man began to play his part in the world's history.

At a subsequent stage a new factor comes into play to still further complicate the situation. All settled nations tend in course of time to become traders as well as agriculturists. Beginning in barter and exchange among themselves and for their own convenience, the barter gradually expands until it becomes commerce with neighbouring and even far-distant peoples. A separate class of merchants come into being who trade for profit. Articles are no longer primarily made or grown for the use of the people themselves, but for sale and for export to other lands. By this means a second wealthy class is evolved, and capitalistic production for profit is set up. In the earlier stages of the world's history, and particularly in the Republics and Empires of the East, most of the work for the capitalist, as well as for the large land-owning class, was done by slaves. Prisoners of war, or poor people unable to pay their debts, were permitted to live on condition that they agreed to forfeit every human right. Even in the great free Republics of Greece and Rome nearly all the manual labour was done by nameless Helots who had no rights of any kind, were paid no wages, were in some cases flogged

every day for offences which they might
commit; might be put to death at the will of
their master, were not permitted to know
their own children, were placed even by great
philosophers and reformers like Solon and
Lycurgus on the same level as beasts without a soul, and were sometimes fed on food
more offensive than that given to cattle. From
time to time they broke out into open revolt,
but were always reduced to subjection by the
most merciless severity. As they multiplied
rapidly, and as their masters were compen-
sated for such as were killed in revolt, these
uprisings were not always an unwelcome
method of reducing their surplus numbers
whilst putting public money in the pockets of
their owners. When there were no risings
the young bloods of the period were wont to
thin them out by battues in much the same
way as rookeries are kept down nowadays. As
a result, work of any kind soon came to be
considered too degrading for a citizen of the
Republic to perform. Even the skilled artisans
and artificers allowed their skill to pass into
the hands of the slave class. Under such
circumstances it is not to be wondered at that
secret societies flourished, and that revolts
were frequent, and that Rome's peril from the
invader was looked upon by the slaves as their

opportunity to press their claim for freedom. Patriotism is not a plant which thrives in the heart of the oppressed. But let it be noted that the slave's dream of freedom did not go beyond a desire to be free to sell his labour. Towards the end, and when the Republics of Greece, and latterly the Roman Empire, were tottering to their fall, a demand for political power began to make itself heard in the clamour for industrial freedom; but, in the main, what the slave conceived to be freedom did not go beyond the right to dispose of his labour to the highest bidder and to have some rights of property over his own person.

If the idea of freedom conceived by the Helot of antiquity had, when realised, been real freedom, then the modern worker should indeed be free. He has every right which his ancient forerunner was constantly risking his life to win for himself and his class. He is free to dispose of his labour when and how he can; free to come and free to go; free to combine and free to strike. He has all the rights of free citizenship in a free State which were enjoyed by the Patricians of the free Republics of ancient days. He has, in fact, all the outward attributes of freedom. And yet he is not free. A stern necessity compels him to give his toil for the benefit of a master just as the law compelled the slave two thousand years ago. The wages he receives for his free labour are often below the limit of bare subsistence. At the lower end of the modern industrial scale there are millions whose lot in life can be no better than was that of the average slave, and must be much worse than was that of those slaves who were owned by a moderately humane master. The slave-owner was under obligation to provide food and shelter of some kind for his human chattels, and would find it to be in his own interest, apart from humane motives altogether, to keep them in good physical condition. The free workman of to-day has to provide his own food and shelter out of such scanty pittance as he can extract from a labour market in a state of chronic overcrowding, the supply always exceeding the demand. The form of freedom for which the Helot longed and fought, and which his modern prototype has won, has proved to be Dead Sea fruit. To the eye of hope it seemed fair, but when put to the test of eating, it turns out to be ashes. In a word, the workman is finding out that he has but exchanged one form of serfdom for another, and that the necessity of hunger is an even more cruel scourge than was the thong of the Roman taskmaster.

There are, however, circumstances in favour of the modern worker which give him a great advantage over his prototype of bygone days. Having proved the hollowness of the kind of freedom for which the slave yearned, he is to that extent nearer the true solution of the problem of the ages. Every illusion dispelled is a milestone passed on the road towards liberty. The vision of freedom is an ever expanding conception of life and its possibilities. Its evolution, like that of every other growth, can only proceed by stages from the crude and the immature to the more and more perfected. The slave dreams of emancipation; the emancipated workman of citizenship; the enfranchised citizen of Socialism, the Socialist of Communism. It is hopeless to expect that a people who are in the full enjoyment of political liberty will be content to continue for ever in a state of industrial servitude. Socialism represents the same principle in industry which Radicalism represented in politics—Equality. The workman who is a fully enfranchised Citizen of the State is a veritable Helot in the workshop. Obviously this state of things cannot go on for ever. He will use the political freedom which his fathers won for him to win industrial freedom for his children. That is the real inward meaning of the rise of the Labour party.

To this it may be retorted that the workman in his organised capacity as a trade unionist is able to regulate and control the terms and conditions of his employment. This is true within limits in certain well-organised trades, but to understand the full bearing of the retort the limitations within which it is true require to be carefully kept in mind. In fixing a rate of pay a trade union can do a great deal, but it has little if any control over the circumstances which in the final resort decide the workman's earnings. In most of the skilled trades and occupations the unions have succeeded in fixing a standard rate of wages which is recognised by the employers. In mining a certain Minimum wage rate has been fixed, and no matter what the state of trade the masters require to pay that minimum rate so long as the agreement lasts. So far so good, but we must look behind the wage agreement to learn the helplessness of the workman. Take mining: so long as the iron trades of the world are brisk there is a demand for coal and the miner is fully employed, but when the iron trade slackens the demand for coal falls off and the miner goes upon short time. His minimum wage may be honourably paid in terms of the contract for the days on which he is employed, but he may only be employed half time, an experience I regret to say only too common in mining districts. He thus finds his income cut down by one half, and his union is powerless to do anything on his behalf. Neither he nor his union had any hand in shaping the circumstances which led to his being fully employed, nor has he or it any control over those which cut his earnings down by one half. He feels himself to be under the sway of forces which work quite without his ken, and which have the power to make him the victim of their caprice. Should he complain, he is told that the employer cannot be expected to keep the mines going at a loss since that would inflict an injury upon capital, and once again the workman finds himself up against something outwith himself. This capital which must not be injured is not his, he neither owns nor controls it, but its claims to consideration have priority over his. If he is of an inquiring turn of mind he may discover for himself that capital must be a plant of healthy growth, since in a single century it has increased its bulk to eighteen times its former size ; that every improvement in machinery increases the earning power of capital without materially bettering his lot in life. It is a fact attested by the late Professor Thorold Rogers that whereas in the days of Henry III.—that is, some six hundred years ago—and ere yet a single power machine of any kind had been thought of, an agricultural labourer received wages which measured by the present-day standard of value were equal to £154 a year of our money, and a carpenter or mason £220, whereas now, when production of all kinds, save perhaps agriculture, has been increased an hundredfold, the representatives of the same classes only receive £30 and £100 respectively. Further, it is indisputable that the tendency is for capital to congregate in an ever-lessening number of hands. Twelve families own one half of the whole area of Scotland. In the United States of America, where capitalism has reached its fullest development, *one per cent. of the population owns ninety-nine per cent. of the wealth*. Great Britain has not quite reached the same degree of wealth concentration, but the process is going on here also. During the first six years of this century forty-six persons died in Great Britain whose estates had an aggregate value of £78,000,000. During the sixteen years ending in 1906 no fewer than 750 separate trading firms in Great Britain merged themselves into fifty-one great Trusts, with a total capital of £170,000,000 sterling. The same process is going on in every industrial country. What we are witnessing now in trade and commerce is not the individual manufacturer or trader bidding for a reasonable share of the world's trade, but great masses of capital massed together like the forces of modern warfare, clashing and contending for supremacy with a force and shock which betimes shakes the world. In this Titanic conflict the small capitalist is pounded to powder by the clubs of the mighty giants of finance whilst the workman and his interests are too insignificant to be even remembered. Many of the modern Trusts already are, and most soon will be, international in their operations, and have a monopoly more or less of the article which they produce. Should the workpeople employed by the combine in any particular country prove refractory or show any inclination to rebel, the works there can be shut down for repairs for a month or six weeks, at the end of which time the refractory workers have been made tame enough by hunger. Meanwhile the orders are being supplied by working overtime in some other country where the Trust has works and the cost of the stoppage can be met by a very small increase in the cost to the consumer. This is no fanciful imaginary picture of what

F

may happen, but a sober statement of what has already happened on several occasions and been threatened in several others. Clearly the Trade Union cannot stand up against forces so closely knit, so far-reaching and so omnipotent as those of the International Trust. The workman who sups daily in the presence of the gaunt wolf Poverty has to be careful lest it fall upon and devour him; the millionaire at the head of the Trust who can reckon upon an assured return of from fifty to one hundred per cent. upon his investments, which may mean from one million to five millions pounds a year for him, has no such fear. With hunger for an ally, he can afford to smile at his workman's discontent.

In another direction also the trade union falls short of meeting the circumstances of modern industry. I refer to the increasing evil of unemployment. In the best of times the average for the skilled trades is 3 per cent. out of work, rising to 8 per cent. in bad times. In certain trades connected with shipbuilding the percentage rises to over 14, and goes even higher in the unskilled occupations. The most which the trade union can do in these cases is to provide a small out-of-work benefit to tide the unfortunate member over until trade again takes a turn for the better. When 5 per cent.

of the skilled artisans are out of work it is a safe assumption that a much larger proportion are only working short time. Here obviously nothing that the workman can do can be of much avail; there is no "demand" for his labour, and so there is nothing for it but to kill time as best he may until a "demand" arises. To use Carlyle's figure he, like long-eared Midas, is reduced to the point of starvation surrounded by the wealth which his own touch has called into being. There is surplus food and raiment and fuel stored up all around him, and he is suffering from lack of all three, but, like the victim of some uncanny spell, he cannot reach that which he most needs. Tantalus must have been intended to represent the strong clever willing man out of work and starving in the midst of plenty.

Such are some of the more outstanding features of modern industrialism for which the workman hitherto has been unable to find a remedy, for which he has been expressly and explicitly told by his political and economic guides there can be no remedy but only palliatives. Hitherto he has believed them, and gone on suffering and enduring as best he might. Now he is beginning to see that were he master and owner of capital and of land he would no longer be at the mercy of a blind bloodless force outside himself which at present he cannot control, and he thinks of using the State to aid him in acquiring this mastery and ownership. Herein we have the beginning of conscious Socialism.

This generation has grown up ignorant of the fact that Socialism is as old as the race and has never been without its witness. Ere civilisation dawned upon the world, primitive man was living his rude Communistic life, sharing all things in common with every member of his tribe or gens and bringing forth the rudiments of the emotional, the ethical and the artistic faculties. Later when the race lived in villages and ere yet towns or cities had been built, Man, the Communist, moved about among the communal flocks and herds on communal land. The peoples who have carved their names most deeply on the tables of human story all set out on their conquering career as Communists, and their downward path begins with the day when they finally turned away from it and began to gather personal possessions. Every popular movement of the past seven hundred years has been a Socialist movement at bottom. The peasants on the Continent of Europe were, as we have already seen, first fired to enter upon their thirty years' war by Communists; the peasants' revolt in England was led by a Communist; in the struggle against the divine right of kings, which ended in the establishment of the Cromwellian Commonwealth, a strong Communist sect strove mightily to make Communism the policy of the new order.   Liberty, Equality, Fraternity was the slogan which roused the people of France to their mighty effort for freedom.   The towns which made great the name of Italy were communal, as were also the towns of England in the days of their power.   When the old civilisations were putrefying, the still small voice of Jesus the Communist stole over the earth like a soft refreshing breeze carrying healing wherever it went.   When Capitalism was in process of converting England into a veritable hell, it was Robert Owen the Communist who gave his fortune and his life in an effort to save her people from destruction. When the hell had been made and the Chartist movement was in full swing, its leaders were Socialists almost to a man, as had been those of the Radical movement before them.   It was fear of Socialism much more than of Radicalism which led to the Peterloo massacre.   When Radicalism with its arid gospel of selfishness was blatant with the joy of triumph, the imposing form of William Morris the Communist stood lonely and grand like a beacon on a mighty rock in the midst of a storm-tossed sea warning the people of England of the danger towards which they were heading. So that it may truly be said of Socialism that in no period of the world's history has it been without its witness, nor has there ever been any rising of the people which was not enthused and inspired by its principles. And now, in the International Socialist movement we are at last in the presence of a force which is gathering unto itself the Rebel spirits of all lands and uniting them into a mighty host to do battle, not for the triumph of a sect, or of a race, but for the overthrow of a system which has filled the world with want and woe. Workers of the world unite, wrote Karl Marx; you have a world to win, and nothing to lose but your chains. And they are uniting under the crimson banner of a world-embracing principle which knows nor sect, nor creed, nor race, and which offers new life and hope to all created beings—the glorious Gospel of Socialism.

CHAPTER VIII

SUMMARY AND CONCLUSION

FROM Amœba to Man there has been a steady and more or less continuous progress. Some power has been at work seeking to make life perfect; sometimes acting through the pressure of hard circumstance, at others weaning life onwards to new heights of development; now bringing forth the tooth and claw, and, anon, the wondrous mother-love. Evolution may explain the process which has been at work; it does not explain the motive power which set the process in motion. That still remains hidden from our ken, but that it exists is no longer denied by even the most materialistic of our scientists. There must be some principle of beauty and perfection in the Universe towards which all creation is reaching out and seeking to attain. How otherwise account for the wealth of beauty of form and colour which everywhere meets the eye? To say that all the charm, all the sweet and holy influence of Nature, is the product of blind materialistic unguided force is, to me at least, unthinkable. I cannot bring myself to admit that hatred, hunger, and fear have been the only, or even the greatest, factors in the evolution of love and the moral faculties. Dead matter must have remained dead matter for all time had not the spirit of life been breathed into it. Whence came it? Not from matter, for that is lifeless. And so I claim that the Socialist, even when working as he necessarily does at present mainly, though not by any means altogether, in the realm of material things, is the human agent consciously co-operating with that great principle of growth and development which, for lack of a better term, we call the Divine Life, and assisting it to find higher and fuller expression in the human race. And this same spirit of progress will continue at work under Socialism, only at a greatly accelerated pace. Combination and Co-operation, not Individualism and Competition, are the means by which progress from the lower to the higher forms of life is achieved, a fact now admitted by all leading scientists and naturalists, and by none more so than by Darwin himself. If Socialism meant, as its opponents say it would, stagnation, then it would fail, and the Socialist State would have to give

way to one more adapted to the needs of
the race. There can be no finality, even in
Socialism. There is no thing over which *finis*
is written anywhere in life. Either we are
going forward or we are being driven back.
There is no such thing as standing still.
Movement and change are of the very essence
of life. Socialism we believe to be the next
step in the evolution of that form of State
which will give the individual the fullest and
freest room for expansion and development.
State Socialism, with all its drawbacks, and
these I frankly admit, will prepare the way
for free Communism in which the rule, not
merely the law of the State, but the rule
of life will be—From each according to his
ability, to each according to his needs. Great
philanthropic agencies, so much belauded by
anti-Socialists, are but the promise of these
better times. The same spirit which leads
the philanthropist to give time and money for
the amelioration of the lot of the poor will,
in the days to come when it is more developed,
lead the same type of person to spend their
strength and to find their highest good in
ministering to the needs of the common-
weal. Change of some kind there must be
in our Social and Industrial Economy. A
Communistic spirit germinates in people herded

together in cities, massed together in factories, and thus made to feel a oneness of interest in their Civic and industrial relationship.

But whilst this is so, our form of property-owning remains individualistic. When property was widely distributed and all possessed some, the fact of it being privately owned was a small matter and one from which no great harm accrued. Now when land is held in the form of large estates and capital in great masses, the result is the oppression of the people. Whilst everything else has changed, the form in which property is held has remained stationary. It is this fact which explains why our Civilisation rests on a Helot class which is compelled to give its whole time and talent to the owners of property in exchange for a precarious supply of the barest necessaries of life, and whose greatest concern is where the next meal is to come from. It is this condition of things which Socialism proposes to remedy.

If, as Herbert Spencer said, life means internal correspondence to external environment, then Socialism or decay are the alternatives we have to face. What we have at present is an altruistic spirit struggling against an individualistic environment. The change which the Socialist seeks is to make the material environment correspond to the ethical spirit. Progress cannot for ever be confined by the cerements of a dead past. Unless the Social quagmire of Poverty can be cleansed, its foul miasma will poison the blood of the body politic and produce decay and death.

We have seen how in our own country the boundaries of freedom have been widening with the progress of the ages. The slave of a thousand years ago, with no more right than the swine he tended, has fought his way upward through Serfdom to Citizenship. The modern workman is theoretically the equal in the eye of the law of every other class. His vote carries equal weight in the ballot box with that of the millionaire who employs him; he is as free to worship when and how he pleases as the noblest baron; his rights are in all respects the same as theirs. Combination and energy have raised him to where he now stands. But his task is not yet finished; the long drawn out struggle is not yet over. There is one more battle to be fought, one more fortress to be assailed ere he stands within the charmed circle of perfect equality. He has yet to overcome property and win economic freedom. When he has made property his servant, not his master, he will literally have put all his enemies under his feet. He will also have proved his fitness to survive as being the best fitted to live. He is better equipped for the struggle than ever were any of those who have gone before. Each position won has been a vantage ground from which to conduct the next onslaught.

Darwinism, with its creed of a pitiless struggle for existence in which the scrupulous were trampled out of life, harmonised completely with, and for a time appeared to give new life to, the Manchester School of Economics, whose conception of Society as a heartless mass of warring units, each intent upon the destruction of its neighbour, had led to results quite as appalling as those depicted by Darwin in the lower realms of life : the public conscience was beginning to revolt against an order of things which seemed so inhuman when Darwin stepped to the front with a theory which seemed to justify every cruelty as being part of the price which had to be paid for progress. It was in the early eighties that what came to be known as Darwinism thus gave a fillip to the competitive system by appearing to stamp it with the sign manual of scientific approval. The doctrine of the struggle for existence and survival of the fittest was eagerly seized hold of and put to uses for which the writings of Darwin himself gave no sanction. His tentative statements and deductions from the facts of life, as he saw them, were hailed as *ex cathedra* utterances from which there could be no appeal. Because hunger appeared to be the spur which led the lower forms of life to struggle and compete with each other for subsistence, therefore, it was argued, it was necessary to retain hunger as the spur wherewith to keep mankind on the move. The struggle for existence was emphasised as though it were the whole law of life. The greater fact that life did not depend upon struggle but upon adaptation to environment, was lightly slurred over. The Darwinian apologists for Capitalism made little if any reference to the fact that no matter how fierce the struggle, life could not be kept alive unless it could be made to harmonise with its environment. They tried to conceal the fact that the survival of the fittest only meant, and was only intended to mean, that that form of life flourished and survived best which was most in harmony with its surroundings; and that the fittest did not necessarily mean the best, but only those best equipped for the conditions in which they found themselves. Now it is seen that neither the doctrine of the struggle for existence nor that of the

survival of the fittest lends the slightest countenance to modern industrial conditions. In
nature bird and beast are free to seek and
take food and shelter wherever these are to
be found; in modern Society man must find
some one to give him work wherewith he may
earn wages before he is entitled to either
food or shelter, and before this one fact the
whole arguments so laboriously built up by the
so-called Darwinists falls to pieces. Darwin
stated emphatically that "those communities
which included the greatest number of the
most *sympathetic* members would flourish
best," and in so stating he conceded the
whole case for which the Socialist is contending. It is sympathetic association and
not individualistic competition which makes for
progress and the improvement of the race.

Letourneau tells us that the ambition of
the very earliest man was to eat and not to
be eaten. The issue does not seem to have
changed much in the millions of years which
have elapsed since this was the victory song
of the successful combatant. The next issue
probably was to kill and not to be killed,
followed by to enslave and not to be enslaved.
To-day it takes no higher form than to cheat
and not to be cheated. That, however, cannot
be the last word in the vocabulary of progress.

Surely it is reasonable to hope that a day will dawn in which a desire to serve rather than to be served shall be the spur which shall drive men onward to noble deeds.

Whatever differences there may be in the International Socialist Movement concerning the tactics to be pursued in achieving Socialism, there is perfect agreement on two leading points of principle: hostility to Militarism in all its forms and to war as a method of settling disputes between nations is the first. In countries where the Socialist parties are a real influence in the councils of the nation, the war spirit is suffering appreciable eclipse. It would, for instance, be a difficult task, and one yearly becoming more so, for the rulers of say France and Germany, to again embroil these two nations in war with each other. Probably the first effective service to which the growing forces of International Socialism will be put will be to make war upon war. The Holy Alliance which Socialism is achieving is not that of crowned heads but of horny hands, and therein lies the only real hope there is of peace on earth. The other point of agreement concerns the essential principle of Socialism. In one form or another public must be substituted for private ownership and control of land and capital. Whether this result is to be attained by State Socialism, or by free voluntary association, like our Co-operative movement, or, as seems most likely, a combination of both, is a point upon which a healthy difference of opinion may well exist; but the difference concerns the method to be employed, not the end itself, upon which all are agreed, viz., that the useful classes must own the tools wherewith they labour and be free to enjoy the full produce resulting from their labour.

To dogmatise about the form which the Socialist State shall take is to play the fool. That is a matter with which we have nothing whatever to do. It belongs to the future, and is a matter which posterity alone can decide. The most we can hope to do is to make the coming of Socialism possible in the full assurance that it will shape itself aright when it does come. We have seen how mankind when left free has always and in all parts of the world naturally turned to Communism. That it will do so again is the most likely forecast of the future which can be made, and the great industrial organisations, the Trades Unions, the Co-operative Movement, the Friendly Orders, the Socialist Organisations and the Labour Party are each and all developing the feeling of solidarity and of mutual aid which will make the inauguration of Communism a comparatively easy task as the natural successor to State Socialism.

As for progress and development under Socialism, these may be safely left to care for themselves. What necessity does for the lower orders of creation, man's reasoning powers will be equal to accomplishing for the highest. Already we have abundant testimony to support this point of view. It would probably take Nature, unaided by man, a thousand years, working along the lines of necessity and natural selection, to so improve the breed of cattle as to increase the yield of milk per cow from 526 to 826 gallons a year, the larger yield being of better quality and costing no more to produce than the smaller. This, however, is what Mr. John Speir, a well-known cattle breeder, has succeeded in doing in his own lifetime.

The average yield of wheat in Great Britain is 28 bushels to the acre sown. Experiments at Rothamstead show that 38 bushels can be got quite as easily if only the proper methods be adopted, whilst on allotment farms the yield is from 40 to 57 bushels per acre. One single grain of barley planted by Major Hallett near Brighton, the result of crossing and selection, yielded 110 separate ears containing from 5000 to 6000 grains. An ordinary barley stalk only carries from two to four ears carrying about 65 grains each. Similar experiments obtained equally remarkable results from wheat. Again, the average yield of potatoes is 6 tons to the acre, but by crossing and transplanting already a yield of 34 tons 9 cwt. has been realised in Great Britain. These illustrations of what man can do in the way of assisting Nature could be multiplied *ad infinitum*. The struggle of the future will be for improvement on the moral plane, and competition of the kind we are now familiar with is fatal to progress in the higher realms of development. It is only when the material things of life find easy and abundant satisfaction that the higher powers come into play.

The reward of genius under Socialism cannot well be less than it has been under Commercialism. Most men of genius die poor, a fair proportion of them die of hunger, unless they commit suicide in time. Genius has always been its own reward. The one thing the Genius asks is to be left free to give expression to the thoughts that burn in his overtaxed brain. No really great Genius ever was a business man or ever could be. Most of the world's most priceless treasures in literature and art have been the work of men who, like the perfectly happy man of the Eastern fable, were shirtless. The inventor falls into a different class from the genius, but he too invents for invention's sake. He invents because he cannot help inventing and too often the reward of his invention goes to others. Under Socialism the inventor would be a much more honoured person than he is now. Mechanical invention under Capitalism has as its first and most direct outcome the dismissal of numbers of men and women who would otherwise have been kept employed. John Stuart Mill, it will be remembered, questioned whether mechanical invention had lightened the labours of a single human being. An invention may cheapen the cost of the article produced and thus benefit the consumer, but often a terrible price has to be paid in human suffering. Under Socialism, when machinery is socially owned, every invention will benefit producer and consumer alike—the former by lightening the burden of his toil, and the latter by reducing the cost of living. The Socialist State, therefore, will have good reason to honour the inventor, and will have a direct interest in rewarding him as a public benefactor.

A like reasoning applies to the argument that under Socialism, the spur of necessity being removed, there would be an all-round tendency to shirk work and that production would thus be lessened and poverty be as rife then as now. But surely this is to argue against all we know of poor maligned human nature. To begin with, the weary round, the thankless task of present-day drudgery could under Socialism be reduced by two-thirds and still leave the resources of the nation equal to what they are at present. On the most moderate estimate that can be framed, two-thirds is the proportion of the national income which is now paid in rent and interest to the owners of land and capital. Whole armies of men and women are now kept at work on tasks which, under Socialism, would no longer be necessary. Let those who doubt this think of the numbers who are engaged as clerks and the like, of the members of the Stock Exchange, of the multiplication of small struggling shopkeepers, of the commercial travellers, of domestic servants of both sexes who pander to the vicious tastes and luxurious habits of the idle rich, of the numbers unemployed and of those only partially employed (I say nothing for the moment of the Naval and Military Services of the Crown). Imagine all these set free from the non-productive work which now occupies them, or the no work as the case may be, and merged in the army employed in useful production. Their maintenance would cost no more then than it does now, and each would be producing more than enough to provide for their own maintenance. With land and machinery socially owned, with the parasites wiped out, with the entire nation organised so as to turn each individual's service to the most profitable account, work would become a mere incident in a man's life instead of being the all-engrossing thing it is to-day. And as the workers would be working for themselves, each would have an interest in producing everything of the best and seeing not only that every one else did the same but that no one shirked his share of the work to be done. The healthy human being likes congenial work. It is only when it is toilsome task-work in which he has neither personal interest nor pride of acknowledgment that shirking is practised.

My task is at an end. I have sought to present Socialism from the human—the visionary point of view if the reader will have it so. As one writer has well said : If anything is to be really done in this world it must be done by Visionaries, by men who see the future, and make the future because they see it. The inventor and discoverer must see with the eye of faith the thing he wants to accomplish before it takes form and shape to the eye of flesh. I have not sought to theorise or philosophise. Most of our differences are due to verbal theorisings which homely common sense puts to rout in the everyday experience of life.

> The simple nameless herd of Humanity
> Hath deeds and faith that are truth enough
> for me !

I have not sought to shirk or gloss over the difficulties of my subject. The one thing I ask is that difficulties concerning matters of detail which have not arisen shall not be allowed to stand in the way of the acceptance of the principles which Socialism represents. Everything has had to grow ; the State as we know it is the growth of thousands of years. Electricity, the post-office, the railway system, machinery, have all grown from small beginnings to the wonderful things we now see them. With each new necessity a new development has been forthcoming. So too with Socialism. Once the principle has been accepted, then experience and common sense will find the way to overcome every difficulty which may arise in connection with its working.

We cannot go on as we are. Nemesis is one of the grim realities not sufficiently taken into account in the great game of life. Leaden-footed she may be, and often is, but that is only her merciful way of giving the sinner time to repent. There is nothing more certain in the Universe than that an injustice done to an individual, or to a class, or to a sex, or to a nation, will, if persisted in, sooner or later bring destruction upon the doer. Often too, in fact usually, the party to whom the wrong is done is the instrument used to bring about the overthrow of the wrong-doer. It was not the barbarians who overthrew the greatness of the Roman Empire. The greatness had already departed ere the Huns and Goths swept down upon its gates. Rome in her pristine strength would have rolled back her invaders as a rock returns the onslaught of an angry sea. Ill-gotten wealth and debauchery had corrupted the early patriotism of the Roman Patrician, and idle dependence upon the largesse of the rich had destroyed the vigour of the Plebeians, so that when the barbarians thundered at the gates of the Eternal City there was no force of manhood within to deny them entrance. History is one long record of like illustrations.

Must our modern civilisation with all its teeming wonders come to a like end? We are reproducing in faithful detail every cause which led to the downfall of the civilisations of other days—Imperialism, taking tribute from conquered races, the accumulation of great fortunes, the development of a population which owns no property, and is always in poverty. Land has gone out of cultivation and physical deterioration is an alarming fact. And so we Socialists say the system which is producing these results must not be allowed to continue. A system which has robbed religion of its savour, destroyed handicraft, which awards the palm of success to the unscrupulous, corrupts the press, turns pure women on to the streets, and upright men into mean-spirited time-servers, cannot continue. In the end it is bound to work its own overthrow. Socialism with its promise of freedom, its larger hope for humanity, its triumph of peace over war, its binding of the races of the earth into one all-embracing brotherhood, must prevail. Capitalism is the creed of the dying present; Socialism throbs with the life of the days that are to be. It has claimed its martyrs in the past, is claiming them now, will claim them still; but what then? Better to

> Rebel and die in twenty worlds
> Sooner than bear the yoke of thwarted life.

And let the final word also be George Eliot's,

in the form of an appeal to those who are
hesitating :—

> Nay, never falter, no great deed is done
> By falterers who ask for certainty.
> No good is certain but the steadfast mind,
> The undivided will to seek the good ;
> 'Tis that compels the elements, and wrings
> A human music from the indifferent air.
> The greatest gift the hero leaves his race
> Is to have been a hero.   Say we fail !
> We feed the high tradition of the world
> And leave our spirits in our children's breasts.

APPENDIX

*Consisting of Quotations from Eminent Autho-
rities, and intended to illustrate some of the
main issues raised by the Author.*

APPENDIX

CHAPTER I

SOCIALISM AND COMMUNISM, SOME DEFINITIONS

What is characteristic of Socialism is the joint ownership by all the members of the community of the instruments and means of production, which carries with it the consequence that the division of all the produce among the body of owners must be a public act performed according to the rules laid down by the community.—JOHN STUART MILL, *Philosopher and Political Economist*.

Whereas industry is at the present carried on by private capitalists served by wage labour, it must be in future conducted by associated or co-operating workmen jointly owning the means of production. On grounds both of theory and history this must be accepted as the cardinal principle of Socialism.—*Encyclopædia Britannica*.

The Alpha and Omega of Socialism is the transformation of private and competing capitals into a united collective capital.—Professor SCHAFFLE, Author of the *Quintessence of Socialism*.

The result of the analysis of Socialism may be brought together in a definition which would read somewhat as follows : Socialism is that contemplated system of industrial society which proposes the abolition of private property in the great material instruments of production, and the substitution therefor of collective property ; and advocates the collective management of production, together with the distribution of social income by society and private property in the larger proportion of this social income.—Professor R. T. ELY, Author of *Socialism and Social Reform*.

Communism is the theory which teaches that the labour and the income of society should be distributed equally among all its members by some constituted authority.— PALGRAVE'S *Dictionary of Political Economy*.

Socialism : Any system of social organisation which would abolish entirely, or in great part, the individual effort and competition on which modern society rests, and substitute co-operation, would introduce a more perfect and equal distribution of the products of labour, and would make land and capital, as the instruments of production, the joint possession of the members of the community.—The *Century Dictionary*.

Socialism : The abolition of that individual action on which modern societies depend, and the substitution of a regulated system of co-operative action.—The *Popular Encyclopædia*.

Socialism : A theory of society which advocates a more precise, orderly, and harmonious arrangement of the social relations of mankind than that which has hitherto prevailed.—*Webster's Dictionary*.

Socialism : The science of reconstructing society on an entirely new basis, by substituting the principles of association for that of competition in every branch of human industry.—*Worcester's Dictionary*.

Socialism : A theory of civil polity that aims to secure the reconstruction of society, increase of wealth, and a more equal distribution of the products of labour through the public collective ownership of land and capital (as distinguished from property) and the public collective management of all industries.   Its motto is : "Every one according to his need."—*Standard Dictionary*.

Socialism, as understood by the Fabian Society, means the organisation and conduct of the necessary industries of the country, and the appropriation of all forms of economic rent of the land and capital, by the nation as a whole through the most suitable public authorities, parochial, municipal, provincial, or central.—*Fabian Society*, London.

Socialism is that mode of social life which, based upon the recognition of the natural brotherhood and unity of mankind, would have land and capital owned by the community collectively, and operated co-operatively for the equal good of all.—American *Fabian Society*.

Our aim, one and all, is to obtain for the whole

community complete ownership and control of the **means** of transport, the means of manufacture, the mines and the land. Thus we look to put an end for ever to the wage system, to sweep away all distinctions of class, and eventually to establish national and international Communism on a sound basis.—*Joint Manifesto*, British Socialist Bodies.

OBJECT : The Socialisation of the Means of Production, Distribution and Exchange, to be controlled by a Democratic State in the interests of the entire community, and the complete Emancipation of Labour from the Domination of Capitalism and Landlordism, with the establishment of Social and Economic Equality between the Sexes.—*Social Democratic Federation*.

OBJECT : An Industrial Commonwealth founded upon the Socialisation of Land and Capital.

PROGRAM : The true object of industry being the production of the requirements of life, the responsibility should rest with the community collectively, therefore :

The land being the storehouse of all the necessaries of life should be declared and treated as public property.

The capital necessary for industrial operations should be owned and used collectively.

Work and wealth resulting therefrom should be equitably distributed over the population.—*Independent Labour Party*.

CHAPTER II

What capital does for production is to afford the shelter, protection, tools, and materials which the work requires, and to feed and otherwise maintain the labourers during the process. Whatever things are destined for this use, destined to supply productive labour with these various pre-requisites, are capital.—J. S. MILL.

Equity does not permit property in land. For if one portion of the earth's surface may justly become the possession of an individual, and may be held by him for his sole use and benefit, as a thing to which he has an exclusive right, then *other* portions of the earth's surface may be so held ; and eventually the *whole* of the earth's surface may be so held ; and our planet may thus altogether lapse into private hands. Observe now the dilemma to which this leads. Supposing the entire habitable globe to be so enclosed, it follows that if the land-owners have a valid right to its surface, all who are not land-owners have no right at all to its surface. Hence such can exist on the earth by sufferance only. They are all trespassers. Save by the permission of the lords of the soil, they can have no room for the soles of their feet. Nay, should the others think fit to deny them a resting-place, these landless men might equitably be expelled from the earth altogether.—HERBERT SPENCER.

Socialism is one of the unforeseen results of the great industrial revolution of the past 150 years. During this period man's power over the rest of nature has suddenly and largely increased ; new means of accumulating wealth, and also new means of utilising land and capital, have come into being. At the beginning of the last century, the whole value of the land and capital of England is estimated to have amounted to less than £500,000,000 sterling ; now it is supposed to be over £9,000,000,000, an increase eighteen-fold. Two hundred years ago, rent and interest cannot have amounted to £30,000,000 sterling annually ; now they absorb over £450,000,000. Socialism arose as soon as rent and interest became important factors.—SIDNEY WEBB, Author of *Industrial Democracy*, &c.

The mechanical industries of the United States are carried on by steam and water-power, representing in round numbers, 3,500,000 horse-power, each horse-power equalling the muscular labour of six men ; that is to say, if men were employed to furnish the power to carry on the industries of the country it would require 21,000,000 men, and 21,000,000 representing a population, according to the ratio of the census of 1880, of 105,000,000. The industries are now carried on by 4,000,000 persons in round numbers, representing a population of 20,000,000 only.—Commissioner WRIGHT, *United States Bureau of Labour* (1886).

Let us not go further without a vision and a hope. That vision, that hope, is not of a regimented society, but of a community relieved from nine-tenths of its present irksome routine and carking care. If the individual is to be set free, it can only be in a society so organised as to reduce the labour employed in the production of common necessaries to a minimum. That minimum cannot be secured without the organisation of each of the great branches of production and distribution. Common needs can be satisfied with little labour if labour be properly applied. The work of a few will feed a hundred or supply exquisite cloth for the clothing of fifty. The work for a few hours per day of every adult member of the community will be ample to supply every comfort in each season to all. Thus set free, the lives of men will turn to the uplifting, individual work which is the pride of the craftsman. The dwellings of men will contain not only the socialised products within common reach, but the proud individual achievements of their inmates. The simple and beautiful clothing of the community will chiefly be made of fabrics woven in the socialised factories, but it will often be worked by the loving hands of women. A happy union of labour economised in routine work and labour lavished upon individual work will uplift the crafts of the future and the character of those who follow them. The abominations of machine-made ornament will disappear, and art be wedded to every-day life—L. G. Chiozza Money, M.P., Author of *Riches and Poverty*.

CHAPTER III

We have not now to deal with mere abstract and transcendental theories, but with a clearly defined movement in practical politics, appealing to some of the deepest instincts of a large proportion of the voting population, and professing to provide a program likely in the future to stand more and more on its own merits in opposition to all other programs whatever.—Benjamin Kidd, Author of *Social Evolution*, &c.

But the above [figures showing the productivity of land], will be enough to caution the reader against hasty conclusions as to the impossibility of feeding 39,000,000 people from 78,000,000 acres. They also will enable me to draw the following conclusions :

(1) If the soil of the United Kingdom were cultivated only as it *was* thirty-five years ago, 24,000,000 people instead of 17,000,000 could live on home grown food, and

H

that culture, while giving occupation to an additional 750,000 men, would give nearly 3,000,000 wealthy home customers to the British manufactures. (2) If the cultivable area in the United Kingdom were cultivated as the soil is cultivated on the average in Belgium, the United Kingdom would have food for at least 37,000,000 inhabitants ; and it might export agricultural produce without ceasing to manufacture so as freely to supply all the needs of a wealthy population. And finally, (3), if the population of this country came to be doubled, all that would be required for producing the food for 80,000,000 inhabitants would be to cultivate the soil as it is cultivated in the best farms of this country, in Lombardy, and in Flanders, and to utilise some meadows, which at present lie almost unproductive, in the same way as the neighbourhoods of the big cities in France are utilised for market gardening. All these are not fancy dreams, but mere realities ; nothing but modest conclusions from what we see round about us, without any allusion to the agriculture of the future.—P. KROPOTKIN, Author of *Fields, Factories, and Workshops ; Mutual Aid,* &c.

It cannot be too loudly proclaimed : economic evolution necessarily goes hand in hand with a moral development strictly related to it. Nowadays, broken into the indivi- dualistic system, we regard with astonishment the fierce patriotism which inflamed the little cities and republics of antiquity. But this sentiment was inspired by the very in- stinct of preservation. In the bosom of the clans and of the families interests were solid. Defeat might bring with it not only complete ruin, but also slavery. Patriotic enthusiasm was but the idealised love of property. As economic indivi- dualism progressed, the masses became detached from a *res publica* which no longer had anything public about it. The wealthy, the ruling classes, thought chiefly of maintaining and increasing their estates. As to the enslaved masses, what did a change of masters signify to them? "It is absurd," says Diodorus Siculus, speaking of Egypt, "to entrust the defence of a country to people who own nothing in it." This is a very wise reflection, and it is applicable not only to the people of antiquity. . . . The words on this occasion put into the mouth of Gracchus by Plutarch are forcible and even suggestive. He said, according to the chronicler, "that the wild beasts in Italy had at least their lairs, dens, and caves whereto they might retreat; whereas the men who fought and died for that land, had nothing in it save air and light, but were forced to wander to and fro with their wives and children, without resting-place or house, wherein they might lodge." . . . The poor folk go forth to war, to fight, and die for the delights, riches, and superfluities of others, and they are falsely called lords and rulers of the habitable world in that land where they have not so much as a single inch that they may call their own.

Everywhere in Greece plutocracy held sway, and all at once Hellenic patriotism, that formerly had been made so fiercely keen, disappeared. The preservation of their wealth became the chief care of the ruling classes, who nearly always made common cause with the foreign invaders. During the Peloponnesian war the populace took the part of the Athenians, the rich that of the Spartans. Likewise, during the Macedonian invasion, the rich—the "optimates"—were in favour of Philip of Macedon. Finally, later on, when the Roman legions appeared, the aristocrats again made terms with the invaders.

It was much worse at Athens, a maritime city of commerce and manufacture, a kind of Hellenic England where stock-jobbing, usury, and financial speculations were rampant; where the body social was divided into two inimical classes —a minority having in their grasp the greater part of the capital, which it was their constant anxiety to increase, and a proletarian populace, of necessity hostile to the moneyed aristocracy. The sequel is known, character became demoralised; the ancient and heroic ancestral virtues faded away; the ruling classes subordinated the city's interests to those of their strong boxes; Philip came on the scene unexpectedly. There always comes a Philip to subjugate degenerate Athenians. Then to the brilliant flash of Alexander's conquests succeeded political despotism, and in the end Greece, the glorious, became only a Roman province. . . . Finally, in the last days of Independent Greece, and afterwards in Imperial Rome, a condition of striking social inequality existed. On one side a small minority held the greater part of wealth; on the other was an enslaved and degraded crowd. The first usually inclined to subordinate the general interests to their own particular interests, cared nothing for the common country, which for the rest was no longer common; the others, the disinherited, had nothing to defend, and at most ran no other risk than that of changing masters. The conqueror, barbarous or not, could not fail to appear; he intervened always whenever great wealth was amassed in the hands of a population incapable of defending it.—CH. LETOURNEAU, Author of *Property: Its Origin and Development.*

If this were the real state of things, England would be a perfect paradise for working men! If every man, woman, and child returned as a worker in the census had full employment, at full wages, for forty-eight weeks out of the fifty-two, there would be no poverty at all. We should be in the millennium! Far other is the real state of affairs; and a very different tale would be told by scores and even hundreds of thousands, congregated in our large cities, and seeking in vain for sufficient work. . . .

None but those who have examined the facts can have any idea of the precariousness of employment in our large cities, and the large proportion of time out of work, and also, I am bound to add, the loss of time in many well-paid trades from drinking habits. Taking all these facts into account, I come to the conclusion, that for loss of work from every cause, and for the non-effectives up to sixty-five years of age, who are included in the census, we ought to deduct fully twenty per cent. from the nominal full-time wages.—DUDLEY BAXTER, Author of *The National Income*, &c.

CHAPTER IV

The soil was given to rich and poor in common. Wherefore, oh ye rich! do you unjustly claim it for yourselves alone? . . . Nature gave all things in common for the use of all, usurpation created private right.—ST. AMBROSE.

Behold, the idea we should have of the rich and covetous: they are truly as robbers, who, standing in the public highways, despoil the passers-by; they who convert their chambers into caverns, in which they bury the goods of others.—ST. JOHN CHRYSOSTOM.

It is no great thing not to rob others of their belongings,

and in vain do they think themselves innocent who appropriate to their own use alone those goods which God gave in common ; by not giving to others that which they themselves received, they become homicides and murderers, inasmuch as in keeping for themselves those things which would have alleviated the sufferings of the poor, we may say that they every day cause the death of as many persons as they might have fed and did not. When, therefore, we offer the means of living to the indigent, we do not give them anything of ours but that which of right belongs to them. It is less a work of mercy that we perform than the payment of a debt.— St. Gregory the Great.

Your predecessors, said Saint Simon, addressing his Holiness the Pope, have sufficiently perfected and propagated the theology of Christianity. It is now your duty to attend to the application of its doctrines. True Christianity should render men happy not only in Heaven but also on earth. Let your task consist in organising the human species according to the fundamental principle of divine morality. You must not limit your action to reminding the faithful that the poor are the beloved children of God, but must boldly and energetically employ all the power and the means of the militant Church to bring about a speedy improvement in the moral and physical condition of the most numerous class.— St. Simon.

If the great end of life were to multiply yards of cloth and cotton twist, and if the glory of England consists or consisted in multiplying without stint or limit these articles and the like at the lowest possible price, so as to undersell all the nations of the world, well, then, let us go on. But if the domestic life of the people be vital above all ; if the peace, the purity of homes, the education of children, the duties of wives and mothers, the duties of husbands and fathers, be written in the natural law of mankind, and if these things be sacred, far beyond anything that can be sold in the market, then I say, if the hours of labour resulting from the unregulated sale of man's strength and skill shall lead to the destruction of domestic life, to the neglect of children, to the turning of wives and mothers into living machines, and of fathers and husbands into—what shall I say, creatures of burden?—I will not use any other word, who rise up before the sun and come back when it is set, wearied, and able only to take food and lie down to rest ; the domestic life of men exists no longer, and we dare not go on in this path.—Cardinal MANNING.

Unhappy ones that you the rich are! what answer will you make to the Great Judge? You cover with tapestry the bareness of your walls, and do not clothe the nakedness of men. You adorn your steeds with most rich and costly trappings, and despise your brother who is in rags. You allow the corn in your granaries to rot or to be eaten up by vermin, and you deign not even to cast a glance on those who have no bread. You hoard your wealth, and do not deign to look upon those who are worn and oppressed by necessity! You will say to me: "What wrong do I commit if I hoard that which is mine?" And I ask you: "Which are the things that you think belong to you? From whom did you receive them? You act like a man who being in a theatre, and having seized upon the places that others might have taken, seeks to prevent every one else from entering, applying to his own use that which should be for the use of all." And thus it is with the rich, who, having been the first to obtain possession of those things which should be common to all, appropriate them to themselves and retain them in their possession; for if each one took only what is necessary for his subsistence, and gave the rest to the indigent, there would be neither rich nor poor.—ST. BASIL THE GREAT.

You received your fortune by inheritance; so be it! Therefore you have not sinned personally, but how know you that you may not be enjoying the fruits of theft and crime committed before you?—ST. JOHN CHRYSOSTOM.

In the beginning of the world there were no bondmen; and no man ought to become bond unless he has done treason to his Lord—such treason as Lucifer did to God. But you and your lords, good people, are neither angels nor spirits; but both you and they are men—men formed in the same similitude. Why then should you be kept like brute beasts? And why if you labour should you have no wages? Again, good people, things will never go well in England so long as goods be not in common, and so long as there be villeins and gentlemen. By what right are they whom men call lords greater folk than we? On what ground have they deserved it? If all came from the same father and mother, Adam and Eve, how can they say or prove that they are better than we, if it be not that they make us gain for them by our toil what they spend in their pride. They are clothed in velvet and are warm in their furs and ermines while we are covered in rags. They have wine and spices and fair bread, and we oatcake and straw and water to drink. They have leisure and fine houses; we have pain and labour—the wind and rain in the fields; and yet it is of us and of our toil that these men hold their state.—JOHN BALL, "The Mad Priest of Kent," 1381.

If we define altruism as being all action, which, in the normal course of things, benefits others instead of benefiting self, then from the dawn of life altruism has been no less essential than egoism.—HERBERT SPENCER.

The holder of a monopoly is a sinner and offender. The taker of interest and the giver of it, and the writers of its papers and the witnesses of it, are all equal in crime.—MOHAMMED.

This system of unchecked competition—one cannot repeat it too often—means a prodigal and frightful waste. Some have to work too hard and too long; others cannot get any work to do at all or get it irregularly and uncertainly; others who might work do not and will not—the idlers at both ends of the social scale, the moral refuse produced by our economic system. This system is exactly what we find in nature generally : but one would think that human beings might use their reason to discover some less wasteful scheme. —Professor D. G. RITCHIE, Author of *Darwinism and Socialism*, &c.

At first sight it seems true that character has not been put in the foreground of Socialist discussion ; its emphasis appears to be laid almost exclusively on machinery, on a reconstruction of the material conditions and organisation of life. But machinery is a means to an end, as much to a Socialist as to any one else; and the end, at any rate as conceived by the Socialist, is the development of human nature in scope, powers of life and enjoyment. . . . The forces required to work Collectivist machinery are nothing if not moral; and so we also hear the complaint that Socialists are too ideal, that they make too great a demand upon human nature and upon the social will and imagination. Of the two complaints this is certainly the most pertinent. A conception, however, which is liable to be dismissed, now as mere mechanism, now as mere morality, may possibly be working toward a higher synthesis. . . .

If institutions depend on character, character depends on institutions; it is upon their necessary interaction that the Socialist insists.—SIDNEY BALL, *Oxford*.

The animal species in which individual struggle has been reduced to its narrowest limits, and the practice of mutual aid has attained the greatest development, are invariably the most numerous, the most prosperous, and the most open to further progress.—P. KROPOTKIN.

If we are still reminded that only through struggle can mankind attain any good thing, let us remember that there is a struggle from which we can never altogether escape—the struggle against nature, including the blind forces of human passion. There will always be enough to do in this ceaseless struggle to call forth all the energies of which human nature at its very best is capable. At present how much of these energies, intellectual and moral as well as physical, is wasted in mutual destruction? May we not hope that by degrees this mutual conflict will be turned into mutual help? And, if it is pointed out that even at present mutual help does come about, even through mutual conflict, indirectly and with much loss on the way, may we not hope to make that mutual help conscious, rational, systematic, and so to eliminate more and more the suffering going on around us ?—Professor RITCHIE.

The teaching of reason to the individual must always be that the present time and his own interests therein are all-important to him. Yet the forces which are working out our development are primarily concerned not with those interests of the individual, but with those widely different interests of a social organism subject to quite other conditions and possessed of an indefinitely longer life. . . . The central fact with which we are confronted in our progressive societies is, therefore, that the interests of the social organism and those of the individuals comprising it at any time are actually antagonistic ; they can never be reconciled; they are inherently and essentially irreconcilable.—BENJAMIN KIDD.

The process of social development which has been taking place, and which is still in progress in our Western civilisation, is not the product of the intellect, but the motive force behind it has had its seat and origin in the fund of altruistic feeling with which our civilisation has become equipped. The survival of the fittest, of course, does not mean the survival of the strongest, it means the survival of the adapted—the survival of the most fitted to the circumstances which surround it. A fish survives in water when a leaking ironclad goes to the bottom, not because it is stronger, but because it is better adapted to the element in which it lives. A Texas bull is stronger than a mosquito, but in an autumn drought the bull dies, the mosquito lives. Fitness to survive is simply fittedness, and has nothing to do with strength, or courage, or intelligence, or cunning as such, but only with adjustments as fit or unfit to the world around. . . . Men begin to see an undeviating ethical purpose in this material world—a tide, that from eternity has never turned, making for perfectness. In that vast progression of Nature, that vision of all things from the first of time moving from low to high, from incompleteness to completeness, from imperfection to perfection, the moral nature recognises in all its height and depth the eternal claim upon itself.—Professor DRUMMOND.

Man, no doubt, is very weak: he is still a long way from being perfect. No doubt the coarse instincts of the beast are still alive in him, for he has freed himself from brute-like existence only by long and constant efforts, and animality has by no means lost its hold. But by a long course of steady progress, ever more and more conscient, he has improved his condition, and in future ages he will do so to a much greater extent.—CH. LETOURNEAU.

A great nation does not mock Heaven and its powers by pretending belief in a revelation which asserts the love of money to be the root of all evil, and declaring at the same time that it is actuated, and intends to be actuated, in all their national deeds and measures by no other love.—JOHN RUSKIN.

CHAPTER V

I contend that from 1563 to 1824, a conspiracy, concocted by the law and carried out by parties interested in its success, was entered into, to cheat the English workman of his wages, to tie him to the soil, to deprive him of hope, and to degrade him into irremediable poverty.—THOROLD ROGERS.

Hitherto it is questionable if all the mechanical inventions yet made have lightened the day's toil of any human being. They have enabled a great population to live the same life of drudgery and imprisonment, and an increased number of manufacturers, and others, to make large fortunes. . . . To work at the bidding and for the profit of another without any interest in the work—the price of their labour being adjusted by hostile competition, one side demanding as much, and the other paying as little, as possible—is not, even when wages are high, a satisfactory state for human beings of educated intelligence, who have ceased to think themselves naturally inferior to those whom they serve. . . . The objection ordinarily made to a system of community of property and equal distribution of the produce, that each person would be incessantly occupied in evading his fair share of the work, points, undoubtedly, to a real difficulty. But those who urge this objection forget to how great an extent the same difficulty exists under the system on which nine-tenths of the business of society is now conducted. The objection supposes that honest and efficient labour is only to be had from those who are themselves individually to reap the benefit of their own exertions. But how small a part of all the labour performed in England, from the lowest paid to the highest, is done by persons working for their own benefit. From the Irish reaper or hodman to the Chief Justice or the Minister of State, nearly all the work of society is remunerated by day wages or fixed salaries. A factory operative has less personal interest in his work than a member of a Communist association, since he is not, like him, working for a partnership of which he is himself a member. . . .

But these difficulties, though real, are not necessarily insuperable. The apportionment of work to the strength and capacities of individuals, the mitigation of a general rule to provide for cases in which it would operate harshly, are not problems to which human intelligence, guided by a sense of justice, would be inadequate. And the worst and most unjust arrangement which could be made of these points, under a system aiming at equality, would be so far short of the inequality and injustice with which labour (not to speak of remuneration) is now apportioned, as to be scarcely worth counting in the comparison. We must remember too that Communism, as a system of society, exists only in idea ; that its difficulties, at present, are much better understood than its resources; and that the intellect of mankind is only beginning to contrive the means of organising it in detail, so as to overcome the one and derive the greatest advantage from the other.

If, therefore, the choice were to be made between Communism with all its chances, and the present state of society with all its sufferings and injustices; if the institution of private property necessarily carried with it as a consequence, that the produce of labour should be apportioned as we now see it, almost in an inverse ratio to the labour—the largest portions to those who have never worked at all, the next largest to those whose work is almost nominal, and so in a descending scale, the remuneration dwindling as the work grows harder and more disagreeable, until the most fatiguing and exhausting bodily labour cannot count with certainty on being able to earn even the necessaries of life—if this or Communism were the alternative, all the difficulties, great or small, of Communism would be but as dust in the balance.— John Stuart Mill.

To me, at least, it would be enough to condemn modern society as hardly an advance on slavery or serfdom, if the permanent condition of industry were to be that which we behold, that 90 per cent. of the actual producers of wealth have no home that they can call their own beyond the end of the week; have no bit of soil, or so much as a room that belongs to them; have nothing of value of any kind except as much old furniture as will go in a cart; have the precarious chance of weekly wages which barely suffice to keep them in health; are housed for the most part in places that no man thinks fit for his horse; are separated by so narrow a margin from destitution that a month of bad trade, sickness, or unexpected loss brings them face to face with hunger and pauperism. . . . This is the normal state of the average workman in town or country.—Frederic Harrison.

It is mainly to our industry that we owe our greatness. Now, our industrial productions, so exuberant and so complex, result principally from our ingenious implements and from our external division of labour. But this *crumbling* of mechanical labour has a most disastrous effect upon the general development of the intelligence. It has come from the formation of an ever-increasing class of modern workmen who have no time to think or to instruct themselves.

Owing to this state of things we see crying inequalities in the various conditions of our social welfare and of our knowledge. These are fearful plagues in our civilisation; they are blots which all free and intelligent societies of men ought to endeavour to remedy.—CH. LETOURNEAU.

Ye sheep without shepherd, it is not the pasture that has been shut from you, but the Presence. Meat! perhaps your right to that may be pleadable; but other rights have to be pleaded first. Claim your crumbs from the table if you will; but claim them as children, not as dogs; claim your right to be fed, but claim more loudly your right to be holy, perfect, and pure.

Strange words to be used of working people! What! holy; without any long robes or anointing oils; these rough-jacketed, rough-worded persons; set to nameless, dishonoured service! Perfect! these with dim eyes and cramped limbs, and slowly wakening minds? Pure! these, with sensual desire and grovelling thought; foul of body and coarse of soul? It may be so; nevertheless, such as they are, they are the holiest, perfectest, purest persons the earth can at present show. They may be what you have said; but if so, they yet are holier than we who have left them thus.—JOHN RUSKIN.

CHAPTER VI

It is often argued that the possession of the suffrage is of very infinitesimal value to the poor man and will do very little good to the poor woman when she gets it. What is a vote to those who are in want of bread? A vote is not merely an occasional and indirect means of exerting a small fraction of political influence, but, what is much more important, it is a stamp of full citizenship, of dignity and of responsibility. It is a distinct mark that the possessors of it can no longer be systematically ignored by governments, and can no longer shirk the duty of thinking about public and common interests. . . . There is another alternative, and that is the socialistic. The elevation of the status of women and the regulations of the conditions of labour are ultimately inseparable questions.—Professor RITCHIE.

The restraints of Communism would be freedom in comparison with the present condition of the majority of the human race. The generality of labourers in this and most other countries have as little choice of occupation or freedom of locomotion, are practically as dependent on fixed rules and on the will of others, as they could be on any system short of actual slavery; to say nothing of the entire domestic subjection of one half the species, to which it is the signal honour of Owenism and most other forms of Socialism that they assign equal rights, in all respects, with those of the hitherto dominant sex. But it is not by comparison with the present bad state of society that the claims of Communism can be estimated.—J. S. MILL.

There has arisen in society a figure which is certainly the most mournful and in some respects the most awful upon which the eye of the moralist can dwell. That unhappy being whose very name is a shame to speak; who counterfeits with a cold heart the transports of affection, and submits herself as the passive instrument of lust; who is scorned and insulted as the vilest of her sex, and doomed for the most part to disease and abject wretchedness and an early death, appears in every age as the perpetual symbol of the degradation and the sinfulness of man. Herself the supreme type of vice, she is ultimately the efficient guardian of virtue. But for her the unchallenged purity of countless happy homes would be polluted, and not a few who, in the pride of their untempted chastity, think of her with an indignant shudder would have known the agony of remorse and despair. In that one degraded and ignoble form are concentrated the passions that might have filled the world with shame. She remains, while creeds and civilisations rise and fall, the eternal priestess of humanity, blasted for the sins of the people.—LECKY, Author of *History of Civilisation.*

The various forms of Communism are compatible with the most diverse kinds of general intercourse, but not with one kind—venal love. Where there is no production of commodities for sale, where nothing is bought or sold, the body of woman, like the power to work, ceases to be saleable ware.—KARL KAUTSKY, Author of *Communism in Central Europe during the time of the Reformation,* &c.

CHAPTERS VII—VIII

To fill this little island with true friends—men brave, wise, and happy ! Is it so impossible, think you, after the world's eighteen hundred years of toil, to fill only this little white gleaming crag with happy creatures, helpful to each other? Africa and India, and the Brazilian wide-watered plain, are these not wide enough for the ignorance of our race? Have they not space enough for its pain? Must we remain *here* also savage,—*here* at enmity with each other,—*here* foodless, houseless, in rags, in dust, and without hope, as thousands and tens of thousands of us are lying ? Do not think it, gentlemen. The thought that it is inevitable is the last infidelity ; infidelity not to God only, but to every creature and every law that He has made. Are we to think that the earth was only shaped to be a globe of torture, and that there cannot be one spot of it where peace can rest or justice reign ? Where are men ever to be happy, if not in England ? By whom shall they ever be taught to do right, if not by you ? Are we not of a race first among the strong ones of the earth ; the blood in us is incapable of weariness, unconquerable by grief? Have we not a history of which we can hardly think without becoming insolent in our just pride of it ?

And this is the race, then, that we know no more how to govern ! and this the history which we are to behold broken off by sedition ! and this is the country, of all others, where life is to become difficult to the honest, and ridiculous to the wise ! and the catastrophe, forsooth, is to come just when we have been making swiftest progress beyond the wisdom and wealth of the past. Our cities are a wilderness of spinning-wheels instead of palaces ; yet the people have not clothes. We have blackened every leaf of English green-wood with ashes, and the people die of cold ; our harbours are a forest of merchant ships, and the people die of hunger.—JOHN RUSKIN.

A gradual allotment of the primitive common domain, then an inverse movement involving the concentration of these allotments in the hands of a small number of large proprietors : this is the general formula of the evolution of property. The communal system is destroyed by the individualistic instinct; then the great eat up the small; whence languor, sickness, and death of the social body. It has been thus with the nations which have run through all the phases of their historic existence.—CH. LETOURNEAU.

It may well be the case, and there is every reason to fear it is the case, that there is collected a population in our great towns which equals in amount the whole of those who lived in England and Wales six centuries ago, but whose condition is more destitute, whose homes are more squalid, whose means are more uncertain, whose prospects are more hopeless, than the poorest serfs of the Middle Ages or the meanest drudges of the mediæval cities.—Professor THOROLD ROGERS.

Society, like art, is a part of nature; but it is convenient to distinguish those parts of nature in which man plays the part of immediate cause as something apart; and, therefore, society, like art, is usefully to be considered as distinct from nature. It is the more desirable, and even necessary, to make this distinction, since society differs from nature in having a definite moral object; whence it comes about that the course shaped by the ethical man—the member of society or citizen—necessarily runs counter to that which the non-ethical man—the primitive savage, or man as a mere member of the animal kingdom—tends to adopt. The latter fights out the struggle for existence to the bitter end like any other animal; the former devotes his best energies to the object of setting limits to the struggle. The history of civilisation—that is, of society—is the record of the attempts which the human race has made to escape from this position (*i.e.* the struggle for existence in which those who were best fitted to cope with their circumstances, but not the best in any other sense, survived). The first men who substituted the state of mutual peace for that of war, whatever the motive which impelled them to take that step, created society. But in establishing peace, they obviously put a limit upon the struggle for existence. Between the members of that society, at any rate, it was not to be pursued *à outrance*. And of all the successive shapes which society has taken, that most nearly approaches perfection in which war of individual against individual is most strictly limited.—Professor HUXLEY.

There is no wealth but life, including all its powers of love, of joy, and of admiration. That country is the richest which nourishes the greatest numbers of noble and happy human beings ; that man is richest who, having perfected the functions of his own life to the utmost, has also the widest helpful influence, both personal and by means of his posses- sions, over the lives of others. . . . Nevertheless, it is open, I repeat, to serious question, which I leave to the reader's pon- dering, whether among national manufactures that of souls of a good quality may not at last turn out a quite leadingly lucrative one? Nay, in some far-away and yet undreamt-of hour, I can even imagine that England may cast all thoughts of possessive wealth back to the barbaric nations among whom they first arose ; and that, while the sands of the Indus and adamant of Golconda may yet stiffen the housings of the charger, and flash from the turban of the slave, she, as a Christian mother, may at last attain to the virtues and treasures of a heathen one, and be able to lead forth her sons, saying—" These are my jewels."—JOHN RUSKIN.

BIBLIOGRAPHY

A Selection of Writings for the guidance of those who desire to learn more about Socialism and the Modern Labour Movement.

CAPITAL. By Karl Marx. (Sonnenschein.)

CIVILISATION : ITS CAUSE AND CURE. By Edward Carpenter. (Swan Sonnenschein & Co.)

POVERTY; A STUDY OF TOWN LIFE. By B. S. Rowntree. (Macmillan & Co.)

RICHES AND POVERTY. By L. G. Chiozza Money. (Methuen & Co.)

SOCIALISM : ITS GROWTH AND OUTCOME. By William Morris and E. Belfort Bax. (Swan Sonnenschein & Co.)

COMMUNISM IN CENTRAL EUROPE IN THE TIME OF THE REFORMATION. By Karl Kautsky. (T. Fisher Unwin.)

UNTO THIS LAST. By John Ruskin. (George Allen.)

NEWS FROM NOWHERE. By William Morris. (Reeves.)

SOCIALISM AND SOCIETY. By J. Ramsay Macdonald, M.P. (Independent Labour Party.)

MERRIE ENGLAND. By Robert Blatchford. *Clarion* Office.

HISTORICAL BASIS OF SOCIALISM IN ENGLAND. H. M. Hyndman.

COMMERCE AND CHRISTIANITY. By A. B. Killin.

STUDIES IN SOCIALISM. By Jean Jaures. (Independent Labour Party.)

THE ASCENT OF MAN. By Henry Drummond. (Hodder & Stoughton.)

TOWN LIFE IN THE FIFTEENTH CENTURY. By Alice Stopford Green. (Macmillan & Co.)

THE CROWN OF WILD OLIVE. By Ruskin. (George Allen.)

THE ECONOMIC INTERPRETATION OF HISTORY. By J. E. Thorold Rogers. (T. Fisher Unwin.)

SOCIOLOGY. By Ch. Letourneau. (Chapman & Hall.)

MUTUAL AID. By P. Kropotkin. (Heinemann.)

PROPERTY: ITS ORIGIN AND DEVELOPMENT. By Ch. Letourneau. (Walter Scott.)

INDUSTRIAL DEMOCRACY. By Webb. (Longmans & Co.)

DARWINISM AND POLITICS. By D. G. Ritchie (Swan Sonnenschein & Co.)

THE LABOUR MOVEMENT. By L. T. Hobhouse, M.A. (T. Fisher Unwin.)

PAST AND PRESENT. Thomas Carlyle.

PROGRESS AND POVERTY. Henry George.

THE NEW CRUSADE. By A. G. Sparrow.

Printed by BALLANTYNE, HANSON & Co.
Edinburgh & London

GEORGE ALLEN

156 CHARING CROSS ROAD

PUBLISHER · LONDON

RUSKIN · HOUSE

LABOUR AND THE EMPIRE

LABOUR AND THE EMPIRE

BY

J. RAMSAY MACDONALD

LONDON: GEORGE ALLEN
156, CHARING CROSS ROAD
1907

Printed by BALLANTYNE, HANSON & Co.
At the Ballantyne Press, Edinburgh

TO

MY FRIENDS

CALLED

"LITTLE ENGLANDERS"

WHO GUARDED THE HONOUR OF THEIR
COUNTRY THROUGH TRYING YEARS

PUBLISHER'S NOTE

Socialism being one of the most important subjects of to=day, its opponents and supporters alike need a frank, precise, and absolutely authentic account of its aim and methods. The Publisher wishes by means of this series to put clearly before the public a complete con=spectus of the present policy of the English Socialists and the Inde-pendent Labour Party. To ensure authority and precision, arrange-ments have been made with the acknowledged leaders, in action and thought, of the new movement to contribute volumes to the " Labour Ideal " series on those branches of Socialism with which they are par=ticularly connected.

The Publisher does not, of course, hold himself responsible for the opinions of the writers.

Make England stand supreme for aye,
  Because supreme for peace and good,
Warned well by wrecks of yesterday,
  That strongest feet may slip in blood.
      Australia to England, by JOHN FARRELL.

INTRODUCTION

THIS work is of necessity a broad and general outline. To have supported my conclusions by detailed considerations would have meant a work planned on an altogether different scale from this. That is impossible for me. But I have felt that, as Time's whirligig has compelled us to restate so many political opinions in order to bring them into relation with the altered circumstances of life, the question of Imperial policy requires to be reconsidered in view of the many changes which have recently taken place in means of communication and world politics. My feeling has been intensified by a careful study of what is called Imperialist literature, and more particularly by listening to speeches delivered by the Imperialist leaders in Parliament during the session of 1906. It seems to me that despite their pretensions, that literature and those speeches are practically devoid of any Imperial principle. There is much brag, there is plenty of dramatic description, there is a great deal of deference to the Colonies, there is a wealth of patriotic phrasing in them—most of it meaningless and incapable of being reduced to definiteness; but there is rarely the illumination of an Imperial ideal. When practical Imperialism is discussed, the guiding idea seems to be that the Colonies should be allowed to do what they like. A statement of the Mother Country's position in the British hegemony is rarely made, whilst on questions of morals there is a cowardly shirking of the fact that the white man in the tropics does deteriorate, and, as representative of our British civilisation and political tradition, requires, in consequence, to have a moral standard imposed upon him. Whoever admits this well-established fact of the deterioration of whites in the tropics is generally accused by the Imperialist politician of "maligning Englishmen."

I live in no fool's paradise, however, regarding some of the proposals I make in this book. I know that my discussion of an Imperial standard will be unfamiliar to many people in our Imperial States, and will be regarded by them as a denial of their full rights of self-government. That will happen in spite of what I have written to the contrary, for I have recently had the advantage of reading criticisms on my position by some of the Colonial Press. But I am also assured that many of the most thoughtful men whom I recently met, and with whom a discussion on Imperial questions was a great educational advantage, are coming more and more to my point of view—the point of view I expressed during the Natal debates in the House of Commons —as they grapple at closer quarters with Imperial problems. An Imperial standard, however, and an Imperial authority will grow; they will not be enacted. That is only expressing the idea that the Empire is organic and develops its own forms. The "bombastic" Imperialism (Professor Seeley's word) which flung us into the maelstrom of the South African War is a poor bedraggled thing now, and there is a very grave danger that in consequence of that Imperial escapade the Imperial States may adopt policies and grow into a state of mind which will be tantamount to a disruption of the Empire; for, if the British Empire is ever to be broken up, the fatal act will be done when nobody is aware that anything very revolutionary has taken place.

I am perhaps too bold in associating the

Labour Party with this book. The Labour
Party has as yet sanctioned no Imperial
policy, though in its affiliation with the
International Committee, its attitude during
the South African War, and its support of
my intervention on the Natal rebellion, it
has clearly indicated its sympathies and the
political axioms which it would lay down as
the basis of such a policy. At any rate, all
I can say is, that it seems to me that in
general outline my conclusions are those
which the Labour Party ought to adopt if it
is to be consistent with the principles of its
domestic politics.

I have not discussed such questions
as what is a fair contribution from the
Colonies to the Imperial Defence forces.
These matters cannot be settled until we
know what our conception of Empire is and
how it is to be organised. On this point
the Colonies think one thing and the Mother
Country another, and words are used by
Imperialists on both sides, either in ignorance or dishonesty, for the purpose of
cloaking these differences and of creating a
sentiment which will be useful for partisan
purposes, and which does not correspond to
the facts of our Imperial relationships.

CONTENTS

I. THE EMPIRE AND IMPERIALISM

CHAP.   PAGE

    INTRODUCTION xi

  I. NATIONAL EXPANSION 3

 II. IMPERIALISM 12

III. THE CLASSES AND THE EMPIRE . . 23

II. THE EMPIRE AND LABOUR POLICY

   I. THE EMPIRE 31

  II. THE SELF-GOVERNING STATES . . 35

 III. THE IMPERIAL STANDARD . . . 49

 IV. THE IMPERIAL AUTHORITY . . . 69

  V. TRADE AS AN IMPERIAL BOND . . 80

 VI. THE DEPENDENCIES 98

    CONCLUSION 106

I

THE EMPIRE AND IMPERIALISM

LABOUR AND THE EMPIRE

I

NATIONAL EXPANSION

REALISTIC history does not lend itself to stage treatment. The magnificent hero with whose birth an epoch begins, plays but a comparatively minor part in the delicate intricacy of cause and effect which go to make up the progression of historical events. The creative will and foresight of the individual become the floats which indicate irresistible tendencies of currents rather than the origin of great changes, when the outstanding results of history are patiently traced to their manifold sources.

Nothing illustrates this view of history better than the story of the British Empire. Three hundred years ago our country was a small European state, divided by the ancient political feuds which separated Scotland and England, occasionally launched into the stormy waters of European politics, forming alliances, engaging in the political and religious strife of the time, growing rich, laying the foundations of sea power—but an island with no footing beyond its own coasts. And yet its destiny was fulfilling itself.

At the end of the fifteenth century Columbus had discovered America, and England immediately found the world of commerce opened to it. It could not be hampered by hostile rivals on the western ocean as it was on the Mediterranean, or elbowed by competitors in a more advantageous situation as it was on the Baltic. Portugal and Spain had sped westwards before England, but, as has often been the fate of pioneers, the spirit which led them into the wilderness prevented them from enjoying the riches they discovered there. The merchant adventurers of Bristol were on the heels of the Portuguese and the Spaniards, but happily their early voyages were failures, and from the fever of debauch, of slavery, of exploitation, which fell upon Spain and Portugal, England was saved by its first failures in commercial adventures.

In the meantime the country was laying the foundations of sound national industry. A substantial capitalist class was growing up. The rulers, already showing indications of a love of liberty and intellectual and religious toleration, were welcoming to our cities the skilled and industrious heretics and nonconformists, who on the Continent were being offered the alternative of death or exile. Whilst Spain and Portugal were exploiting America, England was increasing its national wealth, creating a fine type of manhood, and developing a national spirit. It was storing energy for expansion. Meanwhile the glamour of gold and the sentiment of Christian propaganda had faded, and when England stretched out its hand to grasp the new lands, it was with the less romantic intention of opening up new markets for its commerce, and of discovering new fields for its people to settle upon.

From about the middle of the sixteenth century, the pirate admirals like Hawkins and Drake began to scour the seas and plunder Spanish and Portuguese ships, but until the more sober commercial spirit of the Stuart times had taken the place of the romantic character of the Tudor adventurers of whom Raleigh was the last, Colonial settlement was not made the basis of national enrichment.

At first, the settlements being purely commercial, were promoted by trading companies, the nation, or more strictly speaking, the Crown, only playing the part of a recipient of the fees which the companies had to pay for their charters, and, in practice, standing behind the companies as their guardian in case of necessity. On such a basis London and Plymouth began to establish settlements on the American sea-board, the first of which was Virginia, and the most remarkable in history, the New England communities.

In the early history of these Colonial settlements we can study the transition from the old spirit of exploitation to the new one of industrial development and political settlement, and the conflict between the two motives is aptly enough focussed in the work and correspondence of a man typical in purpose and name of the solid commercial spirit of the Stuart times — John Smith. Smith was one of the settlers on the James River, Hudson

Bay. The little community, still bewitched by visions of rich gold mines and by hopes that the discovery of a north-west passage would bring it wealth without labour, was going to wreck, when Smith thundered at it to till the soil, pursue commerce, make friends with the Indians, and settle down. He wrote to London demanding to know why romantic vagabonds, explorers, and gold-seekers were sent to a land which only required carpenters and farmers.

The same process of settlement on the land, after adventure upon the sea, was being pursued in the West Indies, and during the whole of the seventeenth century a stream of English emigrant adventurers sought a home and fortune in the New World.

The national strife of Europe found a wild echo in the warring raids of French, English, and Dutch in these lands, and the conflicts raged whether the peoples at home were in peace or at war. The lands were as yet no man's lands and every man's lands, and upon them Greater Britain, Greater France, Greater Holland strove to swallow each other up.

By the end of the seventeenth century

our trading flags flew over plantations, stretching in a narrow strip from New-foundland to Florida, over several islands of the West Indies, over stations on the West, East, and North-east of India and in Java.

The struggle for supremacy in these new lands reached a climax in the next century. The rival trading interests of the different companies, inflamed and organised as part of the national struggles which were ex-hausting Europe, make Colonial history throughout the greater part of the eighteenth century one endless series of raids, in-vasions, and conquests, whilst behind the din and the conflict the trading companies were increasing their commerce and estab-lishing systems of civil government. The dominions of Great Britain easily eclipsed in extent and importance those of any other state. The trading settlement became a political community. Clive gave us the subject state of India; Wolfe, the self-governing democracy of America.

The process of expansion had not been the carrying out of a policy. We must rather think of the British people impelled by a certain momentum and careering along certain commercial highways, not so much guided by individual will and foresight, as having its course determined by the resistance on the one hand and the facilities on the other, which the road offered.

Towards the end of the eighteenth century the expanded nation became conscious of itself. An economic Colonial policy had been clearly formulated, based upon the current conceptions of how trade enriched a nation. But whilst this was being matured, another result of this world commerce and capitalist industry was also ripening. Liberal politics were permeating the life of the nations. The national spirit was growing, democracy was preaching, the spirit of iconoclastic rational inquiry was agitating.

The custodians of the British dominions, drawn as they were from the classes who had sought refuge on the pinnacles of their ancient rights and privileges when the deluge of Liberalism began to fall, faced the new conditions doomed to come to grief. An insignificant dispute grew into a cause of rebellion ; George Washington became famous ; the American States severed their connection with us. The

British conception of the uses of a Colony led to disruption.

The end of the eighteenth century found the Empire maimed, though its hold on India, the land of subject races, had been enormously increased owing to the inevitable opposition of the native rulers to the equally inevitable expansion of the East India Company.

During the nineteenth century the tendency of these commercial outposts to become political communities, developing self-government or passing under Downing Street control, increased. Canada, Australia, New Zealand, South Africa became to all intents and purposes independent nationalities; the old Chartered Companies disappeared and their territories passed under the control of the Crown, or became self-governing; Greater Britain from being a commercial became a political expression. And as this process went on, Colonialism—rebaptized Imperialism in these latter days—became more and more a question of immediate political concern.

At first the terrible disgrace and heavy financial burden of the war with the American Colonies, the petty worries which the newer states caused us and the risks of war which they often brought upon us, together with the growth of a Liberalism, whose vision was fixed narrowly upon self-government and small nationalities, prepared the leaders of all parties at home to welcome, and even aid, the time when the Colonies would cut themselves adrift from the Mother Country and undertake full responsibility for their own national existence. That was when the nations of Europe, weakened by war, smitten until they broke or were welded in impossible union by Napoleon and the politicians who tried to undo his work, were resting and recovering, or, at a later time, were fighting to get back to a natural condition.

Then came an impulse of foreign acquisition, which in its circumstances and methods repeated with a curious fidelity the expansion movements of the sixteenth century. Cathay was again jealously surveyed by nations whose palms itched to possess it, but finally, Europe, except Russia, swooped upon Africa.

For a time the Chartered Company reappeared, but the Colonial epoch had passed and the Imperial epoch had begun.

II

IMPERIALISM

BEFORE the first Parliament elected by the newly enfranchised borough householders in 1868 had half run its course, a change came over the temper of the British electorate. Liberalism was still inspired by the wants and wishes of a cosmopolitan trading class. It had done excellent practical work in political enfranchisement, in national economy, in international peace, but its ideals were somewhat mean and the achievements possible for its practical sagacity were all but consummated. The base money-making Manchester School, devoid of national pride and subordinating everything to trading profits, never existed —but it very nearly did; and when Germany had fought with France the war which sealed its nationhood, nationalism became aggressive in Europe. The Englishman felt stung. Alabama arbitrations might have been the triumph of justice, but it was of a justice unadorned with glory; cosmopolitanism might be satisfactory to angels, but to Englishmen it seemed to be little more than contentment with being left out in the cold. Mr. Disraeli was quick to feel this changing temper. Liberalism was becoming confused as though a mist had fallen on its vision. It did not understand the craving of the national heart. Peace, Retrenchment, and Reform had ceased to appeal to the imagination of the people. Speaking at the Crystal Palace in 1872, the Conservative leader confessed that he had at one time thought of separation from the Colonies, asked to be pardoned for the sin, and proclaimed his inspiration henceforth to be Imperialism and Social Reform. During the intervening thirty-four years the country has been trying to make definite what was but a vague apprehension of the Crystal Palace speaker.

The democratic movements were not ready to assimilate the changed temper. Mr. Gladstone's mind was singularly unresponsive to the tidal impulses of the national spirit. He followed the inner rather than the outer light, whilst his great political adversary had no inner illumination to confuse him in pursuing ends which were enticing to the majority. Instead of recognising and using the new tendency, the democratic leaders simply opposed it and they failed. Now, after a war which will never be read by our children with a gleam of pride, after a reckless policy of military extravagance, after revelations of incompetence and dishonesty, these leaders have again got a chance of putting themselves in sympathetic touch with the spirit which has been misled and exploited by the Imperialist movement.

The Imperialist propaganda in England originated in a revulsion of the popular feeling against the feeble policy of Liberalism in international affairs, and has spent its energies in leading that revulsion from being a mere expression of discontent to being an opposition to the free trade, the internationalism, the humanism, upon which must be founded the colonial and world policy of a democratic State.

In no respect more than in the unimaginative and unsympathetic way it approached foreign politics, and more particularly the politics of native races, has the Imperialist movement, as this generation has known it, been in declared hostility to democracy. Nobody has laid down with more accuracy of feeling the mind of democratic diplomacy and administration than the late Sir M. E. Grant Duff, who in one of his letters to his Elgin constituents wrote : —

"It is required that we should aim at living in the community of nations as well-bred people live in society ; gracefully acknowledging the rights of others, and confident, if we ever think about the matter at all, that others will soon come to do no less for us."

This has been displaced by the perfervid patriotism of the mailed fist, and in the Imperialist organisation for carrying on Foreign Affairs the statesmen and the diplomatist have been cashiered and the Admiral and General put in their places. I say nothing against an efficient army and navy. I wish to emphasise that the efficiency of these carnal defences cannot be judged by their numerical strength and their massiveness. It can be estimated only in relation to national policy. But the Imperialist cannot see far enough. He can only feel at peace when his barns are large; he neglects the fields from which the crops have to be raised. He counts his ships and his army corps, and all he wants his statesmen to do is to brag about his strength and tell how fast his rival's sands of fate run down. There are no neighbours in the Imperialist Paradise; there are only allies and enemies—if not *in esse, in posse.* Fortunately for the State, Imperialism has not been so successful at the Foreign Office as at the Colonial Office. If Mr. Chamberlain had been at the Foreign Office and Lord Milner been an ambassador at a European Court, the flames of war they managed to kindle in the South African Republics would have been mere camp-fires compared with the conflagration they might have started.

The lack of imagination which must always make Imperialism a danger in Foreign relationships makes it futile in the administration of dependencies. The Native, to the Imperialist, is always a political bondsman and generally a mere tool in white men's hands for the exploit-ation of his country. We subscribe our money to Missionary Societies and the

Imperialist ascribes a rebellion[1] in Natal to the propaganda of the Christian Ethic regarding human rights.[2] We crush out national initiative and responsibility; we debar the native from a share in managing his own affairs; we establish a law and order which the native does not understand; our breath is too often poison to the peoples we rule; but the Imperialist bursts into song because in the South Sea Islands British peace and British ways are being observed. He has never thought over the truth that is in Bagehot's reflection that "the higher being is not and cannot be a model for the lower; he could not mould himself on it if he would, and would not if he could." In moulds of British thought and British notions of excellence the Imperialist would shape all

[1] There never was a rebellion in reality, but a hunt.

[2] *Cf.* Despatch of Governor to Secretary of State for the Colonies, No. 1 in Cd. 3247, where the spread of Ethiopianism is put down as one of the most important reasons for the Natal disturbances. But what is Ethiopianism, except the social and political movement which Christian teaching has nurtured in a race neglected and kept subject as were the slaves who first embraced the faith in Rome and whose consequent actions associated Christianity with political revolution?

races — except when any of these races
become restive, and then he tells us that
unless we punish with the swift brutality
of the native civilisation, our hold upon
our wards will be loosened and our authority will vanish.   In a word, the democratic principle of native administration
is to develop native civilisation on its
own lines—the educational method ; the
Imperialist method is to impose upon it an
alien civilisation—the political method.   As
in foreign policy so in native administration,
the Imperialist, seeing and seeking only
surface results, understands only summary
methods.   No man believes more firmly
that force is a remedy than he who cannot
see below the surface of things.

The same Imperialist defect, manifesting
itself in trade, has been the cause of some
considerable loss of markets.   The British
manufacturer has been so thoroughly con-
vinced that his interpretation of what are
the needs of other peoples is correct
that when more imaginative and sympathetic rivals have appeared on his field,
his goods have ceased to be asked for.
He sticks to his English language, English
coinage, English weights and measures in

his catalogues, and to his English notions of what foreigners ought to demand, not because he is careless, but because he is unable to put himself in other people's shoes, to conceive the mind of the Indian, or live in idea the life of the Chinaman.

For his losses, he turns to external causes. He wants a readjustment of Tariff and Preferential trade, and again displays his fatal lack of imagination by his failure to understand the political and industrial mind of the Colonies. He mouths fine-sounding phrases that are sometimes red hot with aggression, sometimes gorgeous with the trappings of racial pride, but he never tries to discover the value of his words in terms of definite business arrangements which the Colonies will accept.

His failure in trade compels him to turn his attention to exploitation, and, all unknowing to himself, he begins to be moved by the same motive which inspired the Spaniard in New Mexico. He demands serf labour. China becomes a recruiting ground for his mines, India and the Islands of the Seas for his sugar-fields and his ships. He is driven to claim an

economic predominance for his race which
it is at liberty to assert independently
of the ethical considerations affecting the
relationship of master and servant in a
civilised community. His conscience is
not dead, however, and he compels his
spiritual leaders to invent for him some
such justification as that of a "regrettable
necessity" in order that he may serve both
God and Mammon—"regrettable" the sop
thrown to God, "necessity" the homage
paid to Mammon.

Again, this spirit has a direct influence
upon the character of a country's business.
It creates an impatience with the slow and
laborious processes of legitimate trade and
encourages the mere financier and the parasite ; and the financier is the most dangerous
man for implicating us in foreign trouble.
His profits are generally made under considerable risk, as when he lends money to
Egypt; and he is especially interested in
controlling the organs of public opinion in
politics. Imperialism, moreover, is exactly
the kind of public faith which enables him
to claim the protection of national armaments in advancing his personal interests,
because Imperialism exaggerates the right

of a citizen to call upon his country for support. High finance and politics cannot be separated. The financier has often more to say in foreign relationships than the Foreign Secretary and all the King's Ministers put together.

On each of these points the Imperialist movement of this generation challenges the democratic purpose.

As regards political methods and ends, its challenge is equally emphatic. To it, the ideal of national self-government is as dusty an antiquity as the Jacobite claim to the throne. Nationality, a precious sense for the Imperialist himself, is regarded by him as a mere obsession when found in other people. His ideal is swollen dominions ruled by a bureaucracy of what he calls "experts," with perhaps subordinate democratic forms in the background. His state is based upon militarism, and the elevation of the soldier above the citizen is inevitable. The natural result of his propaganda could not be better stated than in the words of one of his own writers: "Authority rather than liberty seems for the moment to have the upper hand; power and dominion rather than freedom and independence are the ideas that appeal to the imagination of the masses; men's thoughts are turned outward rather than inward; the national ideal has given place to the Imperial."[1] It is impossible to dispute these statements, except in so far as they seem to imply that the mood they express is permanent or that "the masses" have found a resting-place on such a political standpoint. But the corollary of the statement is perfectly plain. It is that democracy and Imperialism are incompatible.

[1] W. F. Moneypenny, "The Empire and the Century," pp. 5, 6.

III

THE CLASSES AND THE EMPIRE

HOWEVER we may desire nowadays to describe the Empire as our "white man's burden," or however enraptured may be our hymns regarding its Heaven-ordained destiny, its origin was no more Divine than our greed for gain. The Empire was not a political but a commercial venture. The Colonial settlements were at first factories in the profits of which the Crown and trading companies shared ; or they were exploiting outposts of white men where the labour of natives was used to throw glittering riches upon the lap of European powers ; or they were depôts or plantations for the distribution of European goods and the supply of articles of European consumption. To this day that epoch of Colonial policy survives in cases like the South African Chartered Company, and, though not nominally so, the Congo Free State. Both of these administrations are frankly capitalistic. They exist for the purpose of exploitation, with the native as an instrument; they employ the language of patriotism and appeal to the spirit of nationality only to enable them to increase their dividends and divert the attention of the public from their operations. Just as Lord Chesterfield tells us that the Indian Nabob of his day put up the price of constituencies, so the successful Colonial exploiters of modern times have, both in England and Belgium, suborned the Press, flouted the Corrupt Practices Law, and degraded the tone of both our public and private life.

Even the colony which was to be a permanent settlement of people who were to spread over the land, was an appendage to capitalism. Its markets were kept open for home products by the sovereign decrees of the Home Government; its trade was a monopoly of the home country—in short, it was commercially even more than politically a "possession." No consideration of political or national glory induced the capitalists to view the Empire with favour when it ceased to yield them profits. Then they talked about cutting the Colonies adrift.

The greater part of the energy of the Imperialists of to-day, if they express themselves accurately in their speeches, springs from a hope that the Colonies may improve as a market for British goods, and they worship the flag not as a historical and spiritual symbol but as a trading asset. Practically the whole of the band of gentlemen who by subscription and voice are keeping the Tariff Reform League in existence are personally interested in the higher rents and the increased profits which an effective system of Imperial Preference, involving Protection in Great Britain, would bring them. They are mainly concerned with securing economic advantages for their class. They support the Empire for business reasons.

They also monopolise the Imperial offices. The more territory we annex the larger is the income of our governing classes. The army and navy have always been associated with dominions over the sea, and these forces have been the preserves of the

well-to-do.   In no part of the State has Social
influence been more powerful than in the
things pertaining to war.   The way in which
officers are appointed, the methods of training them, the social traditions of army life,
the pay and the expenses, the class caste of
the officer fraternity, make army commands
an appendage not only of Society but of the
inner rings of Society.   What would become of all these younger sons and possible heirs and rich youths if our Empire
did not require an army or if our army
was democratised ?

It is the same with the higher grades of
the Civil Service.   Gradually these offices
drift further and further away from the
democracy.   The entrance examinations
are designed more and more to secure for a
few Oxford Colleges and institutions of the
same kind a monopoly of these appointments.   These sons of the well-to-do are
honest as a whole, and painstaking as a
rule.   They are the finest race in the world
for keeping in old ruts, and that of itself is
some qualification for the offices they hold.
But they are also the least imaginative
and sympathetic of men.   Nine-tenths of

them return from their foreign appointments without having understood the mind of the natives they were ruling. One meets them in the Islands of the Seas, pining for home, surrounded by English influences. One asks them about native religion—that's not their subject; about native customs—that's not their subject; about native problems—that's not their subject. They come of a different race, they remain of a different race. Their work is mechanical. The failure of our Empire except to produce mechanical results, such as keeping warring tribes at peace, is largely owing to the fact that the Empire is governed by the most narrow-visioned of our social classes. National pride may be a valuable possession, but when it becomes a consciousness of racial superiority it ceases to be an Imperial virtue.

Thus, it is not only in its origin but also in its present administration that the Empire in a special sense is a perquisite of the rich classes, and the influence of the Labour Party on Imperial politics must be to democratise the personnel of the Imperial machine. A Trade Union secretary could govern a province *primâ facie* better than the son of an ancient county family or some one who was a friend of the Colonial Secretary when he was passing time at Balliol.   We honestly think that the Colonies appreciate our aristocracy, but the Colonies laugh at our amiable illusions.

II

THE EMPIRE AND LABOUR
POLICY

I

THE EMPIRE

THE British flag flies over 11,400,000 square miles and 410,000,000 people. One-fifth of the earth and one-fifth of its folk are ours. But prodigious as these figures are, they minimise rather than exaggerate the wonderful nature of our dominions. Every race, creed, colour, civilisation, obey our rule; and it is only when one has seen the endless variety of humanity and clime that lies beneath our flag that one has a glimmering of what the British Empire means.

Greater Britain introduces itself to the wanderer westwards by a French province, loyal because it is not asked to abandon its religion, or its language, or its nationality. He passes into provinces which differ little from the United States, and further west-wards again he discovers a deeper imprint of British characteristics. On the Pacific his fellow-subjects are the easy-going children of nature, some of them only a generation removed from cannibalism, and as he pursues his way westwards, he falls in with the newest Britain, differing less from the old in its ways and appearance than the nearer Dominion of Canada. Across the Indian Ocean to the west lie the unhappy lands of South Africa, where race eyes race with suspicion and where the native problem poisons the wells of politics. To the north live the swarms of India—nations within a nation, races within a state, and as he touches at the various little points where the Empire keeps a foothold, every new day reveals a new type of race, a new phase of civilisation, a new stage in the evolution of peoples. So wonderful does it become that light-hearted Pride ceases to be the welcomed companion of the soul; the soul needs to commune with doubt, so impossible seems the task of guarding worthily the vast and complicated inheritance we have received from the past.

And yet, when one surveys the panorama as a whole it seems to assume the order of unity in its vast range from the political slavery of some of the dominions to the

self-government of some of the States.
First there are the self-governing nations,
like Canada and Australia, colonised mainly
by our children; then there are the dependencies and Crown colonies, like India and
Jamaica, chiefly inheritances from the days
of the trading companies, and now—theoretically at any rate—cared for by us so
that they may enjoy the blessings of the
matured civilisation of the West, and that
we, through our responsibility to them,
may feel that we are benefiting the world.
Egypt, in reality, holds the same status.
Finally, there are the strategic points of
defence and the coaling stations, which
serve as links to join up the whole and
enable it to maintain a unity of existence
against the rest of the world.

What is to be the future of this organisation? Is it to melt as Empires have
melted away before? Is it to be a confusion
to our civilisation? Is it to be a stumbling-
block in the way of our democratic ideals?
Does it demand that we should put on the
yoke of authority and abandon the delights
of liberty? Can it become a coherent unity
distributing to each of its parts their proper
share in sustaining their common life? Are

C

the daughters to cease cherishing her who bore them ? The man who has seen the wonderful panorama of Greater Britain, and leaves it behind him without feeling the oppression of these and similar questions, is not to be envied.

II

THE SELF-GOVERNING STATES

EMPIRE and Imperialism are expressions which must be obnoxious to any democratic party, because they imply a conception of national destiny and a method of government distasteful to the democratic spirit. But time itself has destroyed some of the features of Imperial colonialism which democracy could not accept. What once were subject dominions have developed into self-governing States, and I propose to discuss in this chapter the Imperial problem which these States present.

Must self-government end in independence ? Can there be a British Empire of self-governing States ? Whether there can be or not will depend not only on whether such an Empire is politically possible, but also on whether it is politically desirable.

Its advantages are obvious. From the beginning of democratic parties men have dreamed of federations of peoples to secure peace. "The Parliament of man, the federation of the world" has become threadbare by constant use on democratic platforms; and no party to-day stands more committed to anti-militarism and peace than the Labour and Socialist Parties of the world.

If it be said that the existence of our Empire necessitates the maintenance of a large army and navy, its break up, it must be remembered, would not diminish the world's sum-total of armies and navies but would rather increase it. The burden which would be shifted from our backs would be imposed upon others, and I think we are entitled to claim that an armed Britain is as unlikely to disturb the peace of the world as any other military Power.

Nor should we necessarily regard the armaments required for the security of the Empire as nourishment for the spirit of militarism. It is not armaments that produce militarism but the political spirit behind the armaments. Moreover, a nation which divides its territory will not in consequence divide, but may multiply, its armaments.

On the other hand, any alterations in the *status quo* would but rouse the jealousies of the other nations—as when Africa was being partitioned; and if the self-governing colonies became independent States, the number of possibly militant governments and points of friction would be increased, whilst the gravity of a serious war as it presents itself to statesmen responsible for an enormous territory would be diminished.

There may be some counterbalancing considerations. It might be argued, for instance, with some truth that a great power at a crisis is a bullying power, or is too tempted to base its diplomacy on its arms, but, on the whole, a very substantial balance remains in favour of the view that the British Empire under democratic custodianship can be a powerful element in the maintenance of peace and the promotion of the international spirit. So we had better accept the Empire as it is, and look to international agreement as the only way of substantially reducing armaments and thus giving the national fevers of militarism a chance of subsiding.

The greatest difficulty in our relations with our self-governing colonies which I, as a member of the Labour Party, can foresee, is whether it is possible for the States in the Empire each to develop true to British traditions and towards ends sufficiently similar to prevent irritating interference from within. Is there to be an Imperial tradition and destiny, or is there only to be a State tradition and destiny?

During the debate on the Colonial Office vote on the 14th March 1906, Mr. Chamberlain said, with reference to the threatened veto by the Home Government of a possible Chinese Labour Ordinance passed by a Transvaal Legislature, that the Colonies would not tolerate any such Imperial action, and he supported them in their opposition.[1] Seven days later, Mr. Balfour repeated the same doctrine, only with more definiteness, and employed words which made Mr. Chamberlain's position clearer than he had made it himself. If, he argued, any one Colony insisted upon enslaving its hewers of wood and drawers of water, it would have a perfect right to do so and to request either Great Britain or the other Colonies, if they interfered, to mind their own business,

[1] Hansard, vol. cliii. pp. 1292–1298.

as it was only exercising its right of self-government.

In the bald honesty of these statements we behold so-called Imperialist leaders elevating some local economic necessity—or supposed necessity—for slavery in mines or sugar-fields, above the most precious of our Imperial traditions. The "Imperial thinking" of the Imperialists is still apparently prepared to accept the doctrine that there can be membership in the Empire without responsibility to the Imperial life. This can best be described as Professor Seeley described the old colonial system: "An irrational jumble of two opposite conceptions."

What these Imperialists contemplate is a group of independent States, each one irresponsible for the policy and actions of the rest. But this is a negation of the idea of any unity more vital than diplomatic and mechanical alliance, whereas Empire presupposes a common racial policy, or a uniform political purpose either imposed by authority or agreed to by the allied States. The Imperialist has not thought about his Empire. He has not got beyond the stage of wanting an Empire—that is his principle, and of trusting the man on the spot—that is his method; and he has not yet discovered that his method is miserably inadequate in view of the nature of his aspirations. He has only reached that primitive stage of thought in which whatever action his tribe or tribesmen take is accepted as right irrespective of any standard of qualitative worth, and in which the bigger his tribe the more important does he appear to himself to be. He has no sense of a "British" tradition, or a "British" genius, or a "British" policy. He claims that circumstances alter national and racial methods (which is true), but from that deducts the corollary, so destructive to every Imperial idea, that practically no attempt should be made by an Imperial authority to maintain traditional and racial standards in the administration of the several colonies. He is concerned with men not with policies. If a Boer lashes a black, or shoots him, the Imperialist of the primitive habits of thought sharpens his swords and bayonets to subdue the Boer; if a British Colonist does the same, the person who prides himself on thinking Imperially is perfectly certain that nothing else ought to have been done because "the British man on the spot" did it.

"The man on the spot" conception of Imperial responsibility is a negation of the Imperial idea. It leads to anarchy and chaos. No wonder that such Imperialists, having in reality (however strongly they may protest to the contrary) abandoned faith in the spiritual and political bond of Empire, seek to cement it by trading profits.

But we must not allow them to assume that their "man on the spot" shibboleth gets them out of any difficulty. What "man on the spot"? Sir William Butler was as much on the spot in South Africa as Lord Milner before the war, and, as events turned out, the General displayed far more insight and foresight than the Governor. But Sir William Butler was in the minority, and according to the new Imperialism nobody is "on the spot" unless he belongs to a majority.

Here one discovers another important difference between the methods of the Imperialist of to-day and the policy of the Labour Party. The latter does not in any way discount the knowledge of

"the man on the spot," but it does not
forget that there are always "two men
on the spot," and its task is to discrimi-
nate between the true and the false voice.
It must apply a test. The test of race
which the Imperialist hurriedly applies
at the first sign of opposition is only an
appeal to ignorance and prejudice, because
both the men on the spot are British—
Sir William Butler, indeed, having a somewhat better British ancestry than Lord
Milner. Nor is the test of the majority
in many instances sound; because in so
many of these Imperial problems the interest of the white settlers in committing
the Empire to a foolhardy or unjust series
of actions is so perfectly obvious that local
majorities are untrustworthy guides when
the whole Empire is concerned. Therefore, what the majority test of the Imperialists amounts to is a claim that a local
majority may commit the whole Empire to
a course of action.

The fact is, as the Labour Party would
insist, that the whole of the Empire cannot
help being made responsible for the acts of
its States. If Natal condemns its natives
to death by drumhead courts which every

one knows are absolutely incapable of appreciating evidence or arriving at a judicial decision, and if the Home Premier condones the conduct of Imperial officers who played a leading part in these disgraceful episodes, it is sheer hypocrisy on the part of our Foreign Secretary to threaten the Congo Government for allowing the murder of natives in the rubber forests. If these acts which a majority in a State initiate are to be credited to the Empire and not merely to the citizens of the State concerned, some attempt must be made to devise Imperial principles of State conduct.

That this is essential is admitted at once when we consider the financial aspects of Imperial responsibility. The financial and monied interests which are predominant in the Imperial propaganda of to-day, would be shocked beyond expression if Natal were to go bankrupt and repudiate its debts; and they would instantly clamour for some action being taken to relieve the Empire of the odium of a fraudulent State. But it is just as important that we should keep unsullied the judicial and administrative good name of the Empire as that its financial probity should remain intact.

Another aspect of my contention will also be readily granted in a partial way. I argue that no State within the Empire has the right to adopt a policy of administration or a standard of civil liberty contrary to, or lower than, the traditional policy and standard of the Empire itself, and I base my argument mainly upon the consideration that if any such departure is allowed, it involves the whole Empire. State action becomes as a matter of fact Imperial action and the Empire has to take the consequences.

That this is really so is appreciated at once when the State action becomes a *casus belli*. None of the most aggressive advocates of State rights would seriously contend that a self-governing Colony has the right to plunge the Empire in war without the consent of the Imperial authorities. But with a quickened sense of democratic honour and an appreciation of the spiritual inheritance of race and Empire, it surely is as important to preserve our Imperial standards of equity and civil liberty from what may be the degrading effects of a Colony's policy, as it is to protect the Imperial forces from being embroiled in war by the Cabinet of a self-governing Imperial State.

I do not for a moment disguise from myself the fact that the people of the self-governing States hold such a doctrine as this in great suspicion. Under the old conditions of Imperial rule when means of communication were so defective and distance meant so much, when there was so little going and coming between the Mother Country and the Colonies, and when our Imperial statesmen regarded colonies as the property of the Home Land, the yoke of Imperial interference was heavy and irritating, and those days are only remembered by convict ships, trading edicts, and governor's orders which threatened to scatter across the pages of our history many episodes like those of Bunker Hill and Saratoga. But those times have changed, and if we return to conceptions of a united people, coherent, organically connected, following a common destiny, pursuing the same world policy, we do so in a totally different frame of mind from that which animated the George III.s and the Norths.

The unity which we seek cannot be

imposed. It must be an expression of a
desire already existing, just as restrictive
legislation to be successful must not be a
yoke but the measure of further liberty. It
must come from within, not from without.
That, we now assume. Our daughter
States need not trouble to argue with us
upon that point. Canada, New Zealand,
Australia, South Africa, have as much right
to an independent existence and development as has Great Britain. If they remain within the Empire it is of their own
free will and for reasons which appeal to
themselves ; if they accept Imperial standards and recognise the responsibilities, as
well as claim the privileges, of State-hood
within the British hegemony, again, it is
to be of their own free will. When our
people over the seas accept these assur-
ances the preliminary difficulties to Imperial thinking will be overcome.

No party has more opportunity for allay-
ing the natural suspicion of the Colonies
in this respect than the Labour Party.
The political organisations of Labour and
Socialism all the world over are in the
closest relations with each other. In spite
of many differences in their State policies,

which have arisen owing to geographical
and industrial differences, in spirit the
Labour Parties within the Empire are the
same and their representatives are received
with fraternal greeting by all the other
Labour Parties.   The significance of the
fact that in every state of Australia the
Labour Party is either in office or is the
regular Opposition, and that the Party is
rapidly widening its horizon and is becoming conscious of the part which Labour
Parties have to play in the world's politics,
has been altogether lost sight of by those
who still think as Mr. Chamberlain seems
to do, that the last word which our Imperial States will have to say upon this
Imperial relationship is: "If you interfere when we think you are wrong, it is
intolerable ; but it is not less intolerable
when we think you are right." [1]   To us
of the Labour Party this language and
thought are both antiquated.   They describe a position which does not exist in
our minds.   The accusation of interference does not apply to us.   We think
of common agreement.   The Imperial

[1] Hansard, vol. cliii. p. 1296.

standard is not to be laid down by Downing Street, but by the self-governing States taking on their shoulders their Imperial burden. It is not the " you "—the Mother Land—who are to interfere ; it is the " we " —the Confederation of the Empire—who are to decide. But at the present moment there is not sufficient identity of interest between political organisations at home and in the Colonies, other than those of the Labour Parties, to provide the conditions from which the new confidence is to spring up. A friendly co-operation between the Labour Parties in the Empire seems to me, not to be all that is required, but an essential first step to a genuine Imperial unity.

But we must pursue the matter a further stage. What is the nature and scope of the Imperial standard to which I have been referring ? And what is to be the form of the authority which is to give it effect ? An attempt to answer these questions will bring us right to the heart of the practical problems of Imperial organisation.

III

THE IMPERIAL STANDARD

WHEN the expression "British" is used in civil matters it implies something more than a mere description of racial or national origin. "British" justice, "British" honour, "British" administration, carry to our minds certain qualities of justice, honour, and administration, and our Imperial policy has always been commended to our people at home — whenever they troubled their heads about it—on these moral or qualitative grounds. The Empire must exist not merely for safety, or order, or peace, but for richness of life. Now the task of the democratic parties of the Empire is to establish guarantees that this moral quality will be preserved untainted. If in this attempt any of the essential rights of a self-governing State have to be withdrawn from the Colonies, we need not waste time and energy in carrying on the attempt.

We are foredoomed to failure. Not a single Colony would submit to such a thing. It would rather cut its Imperial bond.

But no right essential to self-government is threatened by the establishment of Imperial standards and the safeguarding of Imperial traditions.

For these Imperial standards and traditions are, in the main, certain axioms regarding human liberty and the administration of justice. That no man can be a slave under the British flag; that the administration of justice shall not be prejudiced or tainted, and that every accused person shall have a fair trial conducted by certain clearly defined processes; that law shall ultimately rest upon the consent of the citizens, may in summary be laid down as the inheritance which past experience has taught the present generation of Britons to cherish. To these may be added what is a frequently asserted claim, if it is far from being always adopted in practice, that British policy is inspired by Burke's dictum: "The principles of true politics are those of morality enlarged."

If these principles were embodied in

a theoretical statement like the American Declaration of Independence, few people under the British flag would refuse to give them assent. But it is perfectly evident, from numerous instances in the history of our Empire and of America, that it is one thing to assent to general propositions, but a totally different thing to apply them faithfully.

The plea of circumstance has frequently been urged to justify these " British " axioms being regarded as geographical in their application. " The ten commandments do not run east of Suez." There are what are called " instinctive " repulsions between black, white, and yellow; there are oppositions between races — the French and British in Canada, the Dutch and British in South Africa; there are differences in civilisations which affect the morality of the relationships between them — the Belgian officer has to kill the wife of the Congolese in order to give the Congolese to understand that the white man will stand no nonsense from lazy niggers—the Natal militia officer must shoot a few natives to show the rest that little Natal is also determined to stand no nonsense—the citizens of the United

States must murder niggers to keep the survivors in their proper place—and Belgian officers, Natal grocers, and American citizens inform us that we know nothing about it because we are not living under their conditions. They are the " men on the spot."

Undoubtedly these troublesome problems which arise when races and colours come into conflict have been one of the most prolific sources of friction within the Empire, and have contributed pages to our Imperial history which we read with but little pleasure now. None of our Colonies are quite free from the taint. The history of the Indians in North America, of the various tribes in Australia, of the Maoris in New Zealand, of the native races in South Africa, is too often a sorry comment on the white man's civilisation, and it presents to the Imperialist writer a multitude of awkward episodes which do not fit in with his panegyrics on how we have borne our burden of responsibility for our native brethren.

I recall these darker episodes of our Colonial history only to remind my readers of the great difficulties which lie in the way of any statesman who attempts to deal with this question of native treatment in a way satisfactory to any Imperial ideal. I certainly do not recall them in order to censure the Colonies, for the Home authorities have known their own minds so imperfectly that one of the sources of native trouble has been the changes in native policy pursued by Downing Street.

Regarding the future only there is not likely to be any Imperial friction owing to the native policy of self-governing States except in South Africa.

The Red Indian is but a remnant, weakened in great part by consumption, drink, and civilisation, hanging about street corners in the middle and west of Canada, a fawning and a dirty beggar. The Australian native is gone.[1] The Maori is no outcast native. He can marry whites, and his blood carries no taint with it, and he is enfranchised. There may be trouble about his land, and the treaty of Waitango and subsequent native land legislation, which have secured him in his possessions, may be felt as a burden by the rest

---

[1] Charges like those preferred by Dr. Klaatsch against the treatment of natives in the Australian North-West call for some active steps being taken by the Government of Western Australia.

of the people, but when this trouble arises it will be just the same as the community has had with the rich squatter since land monopoly became a pressing problem to the expanding State.

In all these States the native problem has settled itself by exhaustion—except in New Zealand. It is not so in South Africa, where it will be a menace to Imperial harmony for some time to come, because the propinquity of different races and civilisations in South Africa is to remain, and is to be an element in Imperial policy.

At first we are tempted to let South Africa deal with the native question as though it were a purely local matter. We think of the 1,100,000 whites swallowed up in the sea of 5,000,000 blacks, and when our kin tell us that their wives and children live at the mercy of the offspring of the men who trod upon the bloody footsteps of Dingaan, we feel as though we should not criticise even when we know that they suffer more from panic than from danger, and that their own neglect or ill-treatment of the native is responsible for what native discontent there may be. And yet, such an attitude is shirking our Imperial responsibilities. We cannot tolerate such a policy of irrational drift. The Empire has a name, the Imperial people have responsibilities. We have prided ourselves on the quality of our civilisation, and if we rule natives by the same display of brutal force as natives themselves use, we abandon every claim we can make to superiority. A bush raid by a colonel of Natal militia, in which natives are shot at sight and every kraal burned, shows but a slight difference in civilisation from some of those raids which the Zulus made upon their enemies when they turned Natal into a desert, and for which we now profess to detest them.

In South Africa, however, there is a second "man on the spot" whose experience with the natives indicates the character of an honourable Imperial policy. The querulous pleas that you cannot trust the native till you have flogged him; that he is constantly thinking of some rising or other, and that you must therefore shoot him occasionally; that you must not allow him to express opinions about your rule because criticism on his part cannot be differentiated from treason, only require to be tested in order to be exposed. They are the doctrines of the domineering Imperialist who comes not to educate and develop but to rule and exploit.

But what is of much more importance on this point than the testimony of individuals like Bishop Colenso is the experience of Cape Colony. There is no colour-line in the Cape franchise, and though the property qualifications and the provisions that prevent men living in tribes from voting may keep so many natives off the register that their vote is a very small fraction of their adult population, they have considerable influence in elections and some constituencies are known as native constituencies.[1] The result has been highly satisfactory both to the native and the Colony.

Before 1854, when the first Cape Parliament was established, the coloured man

[1] The Cape franchise is granted to males of 21 years of age who can write their name, address, and occupation, and who own a house, or land, or both, of the capital value of £75, or who have an annual wage of £50. Land under tribal tenure does not count, and the tribal native is excluded. In 1903 there was a total of 135,168 voters in the Cape, and of those 9343 were natives proper and 10,162 coloured men. It has been computed that the native vote is the deciding quantity in seven constituencies returning two members each, and in several others it is of the greatest importance to candidates.

had enjoyed a municipal franchise in Cape Town, and so well had he used it that there was no room for doubting his right to a Parliamentary vote.   Liberal ideas were in the ascendant and he was enfranchised.

Previous to 1854 the natives were under the direct charge of the Colonial Office and the result was most unsatisfactory, and is to be seen in native troubles and friction with the Colony.   Since then harmony between black and white has been the rule; the natives have prospered, and the whites in the Cape have more respect for them than is the case in any other African community.   The taxes they bear are fair; their interests are looked after by Parliament, and they have sent as their representatives such admirable men as Sir Richard Solomon, Sir James Rose Innes, and Mr. Sauer.   The experience of New Zealand with the Maoris repeats practically the same lesson.

The evidence that the methods of civilisation and that Imperial standards of justice can be applied to native policy in South Africa is overwhelming.   The ten commandments can be applied east of Suez, and though it is easier for some of the men on the spot to disregard rather than regard them—provided they are allowed to use force when they have created rebellions—it is clearly the duty of the Imperial authorities to insist that the self-governing States shall adopt a native policy consistent with the honour of the Empire. In other words, the plea that the circumstances of a Colony in which the European population is only as 1 to 10 of the native justify a suspension of the ordinary methods of justice and the ordinary notions regarding humanity, cannot be entertained for an instant. It is possible that a mistake was made in allowing such a community to become anything more than a Crown Colony, or in giving it separate existence and not merging it in its neighbouring State; but be the mistake what it may, the Colony's claim that it has a right to disregard Imperial justice must be emphatically denied.

A Federation of the South African States would ease the situation, because we may assume that Cape Colony will not allow its native policy to be upset if it has its way, and a federation of South Africa would contain a white population of over 1,100,000, of whom about 600,000 would be in Cape

Colony. We may also assume that the larger the area of a State and the larger its white population the more civilised will its native policy be.

To extend the Cape system throughout British South Africa would no doubt meet with much opposition; the racial prejudices and the parochialism of the Natal majority would oppose it, so would the Rhodesians, and so would a majority of the Dutch in the new Colonies. Nevertheless the Imperial authorities ought to make a point of persuading the Federation that this is its best policy, and should not hesitate, if need be, to retain in a very definite and effective way sovereignty over all native affairs unless the franchise is granted. This expedient is not at all desirable, as it is far better that the self-governing States should accept responsibility for carrying out an Imperial native policy, should boldly face the possible drawbacks of such a policy, should win the confidence of the Empire in their attempts, and then claim generous judgment and effective protection (neither of which would be withheld) if they failed.

Whilst South Africa is being swerved on to the right lines of native policy it will be advisable to impress upon it that those lines are being imposed upon it, not by Downing Street—I suppose that the South African of the domineering School will say "Exeter Hall"—but by the Empire. Consequently native policy should be one of the most important topics for discussion at each Colonial Conference. The trouble hitherto has been that whilst Downing Street has been seeking to apply principles of administration under the guidance of certain human sentiments, "the man on the spot," moved by his parish needs, has been claiming certain impossible privileges. The one has been unable to see the trees for the wood; the other has been unable to see the wood for the trees. The true principles of the one and the detailed experience of the other, instead of being co-operating factors in the creation of an Imperial policy, have only been opposing councils leading to Imperial friction.

The Colonial Conference affords the opportunity for making peace between Downing Street Imperialism and Colonial parochialism.[1]

[1] The recent Natal rebellion (so called) of natives will probably have little effect on our Imperial history, but I

Somewhat akin to the native question is that of the immigration of other than white races into our self-governing Colonies. At the present moment Canada prohibits the immigration of Chinese possessed of less than $500. In reality that amounts to simple prohibition, and the more straight-forward course is not taken because the Mother Country is prevented by treaties from sanctioning a prohibition statute. Australasia is pursuing the same policy as Canada. By a federal law passed in 1901 a language test was imposed upon immigrants, and it is quite clear that the purpose of the enactment is prohibition and not restriction.

feel sure that patriotic historians who wade through the details of the transaction will regret that Natal was not taught by Canada, Australia, and New Zealand that they, as well as the Labour and Radical Parties at home, insisted upon the Union Jack being kept as clean as possible. Australia alone took action which can be called objectionable. That was not owing to any defect in Australian policy but to the unfortunate circumstances of Australian politics. When the smallest party in a State happens to be in office—as was the case in Australia when the Natal trouble arose—it is always on the watch for an opportunity to ingratiate itself with the electors. A weak government gets into a fury, whilst a strong one is still calmly considering what it ought to do.

The motives of both these States are the same. The Labour organisations desire to keep up a high standard for white workpeople, and find that the Chinese and Japanese, carrying their eastern standards of decency and consumption with them, work for wages upon which a white man could not subsist. The Chinese and Japanese emigrant is, therefore, to the Trade Unions of Canada and Australasia just what the Russian Jew is to the Stepney workman.

But above and beyond labour interests there is a racial question. The cry for a white Australia is an expression of the repulsion felt by practically every white man and woman in the country against the mixing of the white and the yellow races. We at home cannot understand the intensity of this feeling. If we could, we should never have allowed, for instance, the mineowners to import Chinamen to South Africa. That one act did more to destroy Imperial affection and pride in Colonies where the colour repulsion is felt, than anything that has happened for many years. Should ever we find ourselves at war with Japan one is justified in hazarding

a guess that it will be Australia that
has dragged us into it owing to her immigration laws or her determination not
to treat the yellow man on an equality
with the white.

How far do these laws run counter to
our Imperial standard? British liberty
has always involved asylum for the
oppressed and for political and religious
refugees, but it has never laid down the
doctrine that free immigration was essential. If an Imperial State desires to protect
its racial purity, or to maintain its standard of living, it has the right not only
to refuse to allow other races to settle on
its territory, but it may even decline to
accept the paupers of the Mother Country,
or of other Imperial States. The power to
exclude undesirable immigrants, to classify
whole races amongst these undesirables,
and to control in other ways the conditions
of immigration, may be exercised by the
self-governing States without in any way
violating those Imperial traditions which
as democrats we desire to preserve.

The ill-usage of these undesirables within
the State, or their differential treatment as
wage-earners, does, however, violate the

spirit of British justice and ought not to be tolerated. The States can exclude Chinamen if they like, but if they admit them, they must not hold them as slaves.

Hence, the immigration policy of Canada and Australasia, so far as it has been developed as yet, concerns these States alone.

The question arises, however, supposing that the Imperial authorities in the general interests of the Empire have made treaties with those penalised races to which this immigration legislation runs counter. What then ? The reply is that the difficulty that then arises is not one of fundamental principle, but of the machinery of Imperial government. The Imperial States should be consulted in all treaties that are likely to affect their liberty of action—not only the State that is most evidently to be affected, but all the States as an Imperial unity. Until our method of Imperial government can be adjusted so as to secure this consultation, the Colonies will be patriotic and generous enough to accept conditions which may be irritating, but for which no one—certainly not the reigning powers at Downing Street—is responsible.

Until the old machinery is replaced by the new, awkward situations must arise.

In one respect the Australian immigration policy is an Imperial and a world-wide concern. If the northern parts of the continent cannot be adequately cultivated by white men, and their natural possibilities have to lie latent in consequence, the same economic reason that justifies us in assuming control in the tropics would justify other nations objecting to the Australian policy. This is, however, very remote, and meanwhile Australia is doing its best to prove that the white man can cultivate its northern territories, and the bounty it is paying upon sugar grown by white labour is an earnest of its determination not to allow the "white Australia" policy to result in an empty Australia.

Before passing from this aspect of our subject it must be noted that this Imperial right of imposing an Imperial policy upon the Imperial States affects the Mother Country quite as much as it does Canada, Australia, or South Africa. When, for instance, our "Imperialists" cried out in wrath because the Canadian and Australian

E

Parliaments passed resolutions in favour of Home Rule, they once more showed their inability to "think Imperially." If the case of the Irish Home Ruler is proved —and Canada and Australia are as able to judge that as we are at home—then our present government of Ireland is not in keeping with our British traditions that government should be carried on only with the assent of the governed, and these States—or, better still, an Imperial Conference—has an indisputable right to advise our Houses of Parliament on the subject of Home Rule.

Australasia might even go further. The enfranchisement of women has become such an integral part of Australasian civilisation and is regarded by the vast majority of Australians as such an essential condition of "British" liberty, that the Commonwealth Parliament and the New Zealand Houses would be well within their rights in passing resolutions declaring that the women of their Mother Land ought to be enfranchised. Whether they would be wise in doing so is another matter, but if they did, no Imperialist could reasonably object.

An examination of what is involved in

applying Imperial standards of right to the legislation and administration of the Imperial States therefore shows, that saving in one or two instances no interference with State authority could take place, and that where interference apparently did take place, it would only be an imposition of the racial and national standards of the stock to which that State belonged.

The treatment of coloured and native races mixed with or living side by side with white people is practically the only serious difficulty that presents itself. For the rest the Imperial standard would be a guidance and control for future policy, and a guarantee to other nations. It would express the spirit of the Empire.

The real difficulty lies in securing the confidence of the Imperial States for whatever authority is to be custodian of the Imperial standard. If these States only felt that they were part and parcel of the deciding authority, that their will was one of the deciding elements and that the decision come to contained in a just proportion their special wants and wishes blended with those of the greater

Imperial unity to which they belonged, they would loyally and faithfully accept Imperial standards. They have lost confidence in Downing Street. Downing Street has advised them wrongly. Downing Street has shilly-shallied. Downing Street is ignorant of Colonial opinion and needs. Above all, Downing Street is the surviving symbol of the era of the British "dominions" and the real "Colonies." The Imperial States will not repose confidence in Downing Street, therefore Downing Street cannot remain the custodian of Imperial standards.

What is to take its place?

IV

THE IMPERIAL AUTHORITY

THE Imperial States are so jealous and suspicious of any authority, except what is internal to themselves, that the difficulties in the way of creating any Imperial authority are enormous. The Crown is nominally such an authority; but the Crown for all practical purposes is Downing Street, and is confined in its influence by the limits of the respect paid to, or the confidence reposed in, Downing Street. This respect and confidence are declining. Therefore, no extension of the authority of the Crown will be acceptable to the Colonies. It is becoming more and more nominal and sentimental. It is already stripped of all political significance except in so far as the sentimental homage paid to it can operate alongside the most pronounced determination on the part of the Colonies to mind their own business. The

Crown cannot be the custodian of an Imperial policy though it may be an Imperial link—and even in this respect its influence is greatly exaggerated at home.

Two proposals which have taken for granted the self-government of the Colonies have been made for the creation of an Imperial authority. The first and earliest was Imperial Federation. This would have created a body which was not only responsible but representative. The second was an Imperial Council which might be representative, but which would not be responsible.

The Imperial Federation proposal involves the election of Colonial representatives to the Imperial Parliament, or something practically amounting to that, but it has not stood the test of time. Men living in London, in touch with London Society and steeped in London influences, even though they are Colonials, and have been sent home to represent the Colonies, as Agents-General now are, could not keep in sufficiently close touch with their constituencies. The authority on which these representatives would sit would be regarded by the Colonies as alien to them, and it could not command and retain their confidence. A

Parliament containing Colonial representatives would carry no more Imperial weight than the present Parliament does. On the other hand circumstances would drive the Colonial representatives into our domestic party politics, and Imperial questions, which ought to be guarded as much as possible from domestic party strife, would be thrust into the turmoil of partisanship. Imperial Federation may safely be dismissed as the first, and therefore unsatisfactory, attempt to create an Imperial organisation for expressing Imperial standards of government.

The next proposal was to establish an Imperial Council. This has taken several forms—an Imperial Committee of the Privy Council which would include Colonial Privy Councillors, a Cabinet enlarged by Colonial representatives summoned to discuss Imperial questions, a kind of Advisory Committee charged with placing what may be called the raw material for a Government policy before the Cabinet.

Although these proposals show a greater maturity of consideration and a fuller appreciation of the Colonial mind than Imperial Federation did, and although they are not open to some of the objections that can be taken to the first scheme, they are improvements only because they have avoided the difficulties of representation by destroying responsibility. But the difficulties of joining representation and responsibility have to be overcome and not set on one side because the authority of a non-responsible Council, however distinguished its members are, must be exceedingly limited amongst democratically governed States.

Moreover, the Colonial members of any one of these bodies would have to live in London during the term of their appointment, and that would so diminish what authority they had in the Colonies as to defeat the purposes of the Council.

The authority which I have in mind must observe certain conditions. It must be representative; it must not lose touch with the Imperial States, and, therefore, its members must not live in London; and, it may be added, each Imperial State should have an equal representation.[1]

Can such a body be created? It seems

[1] The difficulty presented by non-federated States, like Newfoundland, or the South African States, and the question whether the States within a federation, like the Australian States, should be separately represented, would have to be settled by agreement.

to me to be perfectly simple. The Colonies will not give confidence to a body permanently sitting in London or in any one city, but this difficulty is overcome if it be agreed that the body should not sit continuously, but be summoned at intervals. A further consideration in favour of this plan is that it would ensure that the members of the body would speak from fresh experience of Colonial opinion and be under no delusion as to its aims and temper.

It would be quite impossible to elect by a Colonial franchise the members of this body, but the advantages of election, joined with those of representation, could be secured if the body were composed of the Premiers and Leaders of the Opposition for the time being and any other State officials determined upon. Thus the decisions of the body would be supported in the Colonies and the very best guidance given to the authority, as to what limits it should place upon its deliberations and resolutions. In no other way can a body be created which will have authority in the Colonies. It must be primarily a Council of Premiers whose function would then be to represent their States on this Imperial Conference just as much as to lead

the Governments over which they preside.
What is wanted, therefore, is not Imperial
Federation and not an Imperial Council,
but an Imperial Conference meeting with
sufficient frequency and deliberating with
sufficient care upon Imperial concerns.

It has been said that a Conference like
this would create no permanent organisation, would have no executive power,
would not be connected with constitutional
machinery, and that its effectiveness would
depend upon accident.[1] As a matter of
simple fact none of these objections are
real. It would be a permanent organisation ; it would become as much part of the
working constitution as the Cabinet is ; its
executive authority would be real though
not defined ; and its effectiveness would be
as regular as that of any other institution
in a State governed by a democratic sovereign authority. In these matters rigid
constitutions and hard and fast agreements
give less guarantee of permanence and of
certainty of result than loose relationships
which depend upon a common spirit, a common history, a common racial evolution.

This Imperial Conference would discuss

[1] *Cf.* "The Empire and the Century," p. 44.

and practically settle the question of
Colonial Governors; it would support a
general Imperial view of native administration and assume, on behalf of the whole
self-governing Empire, responsibilities for
the subject races' government, education,
and development; it would lay down the
general principles upon which treaties
should be made, and international agreements arrived at, even should it never
become the Executive authority for settling
these treaties; it would express the political problems of Imperial defence, and
co-ordinate the opposing desires of the
self-governing States to have independent
forces of their own, and those of the
military experts to have centralised control; it would discuss and indicate its
views upon that vast miscellany of matters relating to Imperial life from cables
to immigration laws, from Privy Council
appeals to Imperial trade reports.

Its position can be clearly shown if we
consider the part it would play as a treaty-
making authority. At present treaties are
made in Whitehall; after communications
with any Colony which happens to be
directly interested, and when this Colony

does not get all its way, it proceeds to grumble and declare that its wishes have been flouted. Under such circumstances a weak Government or an Opposition desirous of becoming the Government have terrible temptations placed in their way to oppose the Imperial authorities in order to gain local popularity. The recent arrangements with the United States over the Newfoundland fishing laws and with France over the New Hebrides are cases in point.

Evidently this is unfair both to the Colonies and the Mother Country. The provisions of a treaty should be a blending of local and Imperial interests, and as the larger interests rarely coincide with the narrower ones, friction is almost inevitable unless the representatives of the States are brought to agree upon an Imperial policy.

Canada has almost claimed that it is a right of self-governing States to be allowed to make treaties for themselves. When that happens, the Colonies might as well sever themselves from the Mother Country altogether. For, under present circumstances, the authority which makes treaties is the authority which ultimately controls armies. To give any of our Colonies the power to embroil us in war, or to determine our relations with European powers, is to give the first shattering blow to Imperial solidarity.

But if the present Colonial Conferences were regarded as Imperial Advisory Committees, and if, in consequence, there were full and responsible discussions at them regarding our world policy, although the precise events of two or three years ahead could not be anticipated, the general policy of the Government could be discussed by the Conference ; the Imperial aspects of the particular local interests of the Colonies could be impressed upon Colonial statesmen ; the limits within which arrangements could be come to by the Imperial authorities with foreign States would be understood ; correspondence upon disputed points as they arose would be definite and would be conducted by Colonial Ministers aware of the full Imperial aspects of the case; the Colonial view could not be misunderstood or minimised, and the treaty would carry the support not only of the Home Government but of the Empire—even if in every respect the Colony particularly affected were not pleased.

Of course it is easy to imagine how such an organisation would break down. As a

mere machine it is somewhat inchoate.
That, however, is rather a commendation
than otherwise. All that is really wanted
is a formal recognition of Imperial solidarity, as free as it can be devised. That
is the type of institution which yields
best results. It goes not by the logic and
rigidity of its construction, but by an accumulation of precedent and the growth of a
spirit and method appropriate to itself.

If one has a clear idea of the functions
and composition of an Imperial Conference,
he must not permit himself to suppose that
it can be created by a fiat. It must grow,
and it will take some time to mature. To
force it on will be to ruin it. We have
always seen that self-governing States enter
a federation most unwillingly, and, for some
time after they have entered it, that they
grumble at its inconveniences more than
they feel gratified by its blessings. So it was
with the United States; so it is to-day with
the Australian States; so will it be as the
Imperial States enter an Imperial unity
which will be real and not merely nominal.

The important thing for us to do to-day
is to make up our minds as to the form
which Imperial unity ought to take, and

then to see to it that our Imperial thought and action tend to the realisation of that unity. Remote as that unity may appear to be, and suspicious of it as Colonial feeling may seem, one has only to study the evolution of the Australian Commonwealth to see how unity is imposed upon a people almost in spite of themselves. And with the shrinking of the world, the organisation of military forces, the growth in identity of old and new world politics, the imperative necessity of an Imperial policy which will be Colonial as well as British in its inspiration, Imperial unity will come upon us simply as the years roll on, or, one fatal day, there will be a misunderstanding, an agitation, a conflagration, a disruption. And whilst the force of events will be driving us, their logic and appropriateness will be becoming apparent to us. We shall cease to feel that we at home, and we only, must be the supreme Imperial authority; the Colonies will extend their views and feel their identity with a great world power; we both will be inspired by the humility of responsibility which a British Confederation of States must inevitably bear.

V

TRADE AS AN IMPERIAL BOND

MR. CHAMBERLAIN'S facility for dashing off
attractive programmes has brought into the
discussion of Imperial politics a proposal
to make trade an Imperial bond. Signs are
not wanting to show that the proposal is
dead, but at the present moment no consideration of Imperial topics ought to omit
the Tariff Reform and the Imperial Preference propaganda. In this propaganda
words have been used for the purpose of
clouding issues and grandiloquent language
for the purpose of playing sleight-of-hand
tricks upon common sense. I shall content
myself with stating as accurately as possible
what the proposal means in actual trade
facilities and in the opening up of markets.

The citadel of the position which the
Tariff Reformers are attacking is Free Trade
doctrine. Imperial Preference presupposes
discriminating duties against the foreigner

upon the English market, and these duties must not be nominal and for revenue purposes, but must be sufficiently high to alter the course of the world's trade and be specifically designed for that purpose. Therefore, as a preliminary to an Imperial trading policy such as Mr. Chamberlain has proposed, Great Britain must be induced to abandon Free Trade.

This is not the place to discuss the relative merits of Free Trade and Protection as a trade policy for Great Britain. I content myself with stating the issue and with saying that the Labour Party is practically unanimous for Free Trade. One can understand how anxious the Tariff Reform League was to form a Trade Union branch, but since the Trade Unionists of influence and position in their societies who have associated themselves with this body can be counted on the fingers of one hand without exhausting all the fingers, space need not be taken up to discuss Free Trade in a volume dealing with Labour Party politics.

Moreover, we can dispense with this preliminary point and examine the Tariff Reform contention at its centre. Will the Empire accept Mr. Chamberlain's policy? If it

F

does, will it be strengthened in consequence?
Both these questions must be answered by
an emphatic negative.

Let us examine the trade policy of the
Imperial States in relation to the trade
interests of the Mother Country. Only
when we have done this can we come to
any practical conclusion upon these proposals for Colonial preference.

I shall begin with Canada. Canada is
frankly Protectionist, though in the wheat-
growing lands and in the West there is
a strong Free Trade sentiment—indeed in
these parts Free Trade is on the ascendant.
But Ontario and Quebec are decidedly
Protectionist. Working-class organisations,
as a rule—though not a rule without exceptions—agree with manufacturers' associations on this point; and whilst these
associations send delegates to England to
tell us how patriotic it would be for us
to give them preference on our markets,
they pass resolutions at home demanding
that whatever preference we may get on
theirs shall not enable us to compete with
the Canadian manufacturer. The fact is
that Canada is determined to manufacture
as much as it can for itself, and it will

give no facilities to the British manufacturer to capture anything beyond the residuum of the demand which Canada cannot itself supply. It not only protects itself by tariffs; it gives bounties to encourage manufactures.

It is impossible to say what Sir Wilfrid Laurier had in mind when he offered us a preference in 1897, but his Party had declared, in a resolution which it supported in the Dominion Parliament in 1892, that as Great Britain allowed Canadian goods a free entry upon the British market, Canada should reduce the tariff on imports from Britain. A careful study of the somewhat contradictory speeches which Sir Wilfrid Laurier has made on Canadian tariff leaves an impression on my mind that he made his proposals for a variety of reasons. It was a bid for votes by a politician; it was a step towards Free Trade by one who, whatever tariff he was proposing, declared himself a theoretical Free Trader; it was a move in the game that has been played for many years to get the United States to reciprocate Canadian business affections; in altogether a minor way it was a bid for special advantages being given on the

British market to Canadian goods. Since its enactment the greatest efforts have been made to increase the protection of the Canadian manufacturer.

The Imperial trade policy of Australia developed later than did that of Canada. There are three main reasons for this. Until Federation, Australia could not move as a nation; Australia is far more aggressively Protectionist than Canada—excepting New South Wales, which, having been Free Trade in sentiment, never thought upon the lines of an Imperial trade policy ; finally, Australia being remote from Britain, and isolated from foreign powers, tends to develop a sentiment of independence and self-reliance.

But for some years the feeling in favour of Protection has been growing in the Australian states, as the Australian has committed himself more and more to a policy of a white Australia and an Australia where the workman has a specially large share of the wealth which he produces. Those racial and industrial aims of Australia appear to the Australian to require the assistance of a protective system which approaches to one of prohibition for goods which are, or can be, made in Australia. The Australian

Labour Party has carried this idea further
and made it more logical and systematic than
any other party in the world. It not only
protects the manufacturer in his profits, but
insists through Industrial Arbitration Courts
and Wages Boards that some of the extra
profits shall be paid away in wages. Having
thus secured (apparently) the manufacturer
and the workmen, it has turned to the third
and last economic function in a community
—the consumer—and it proposes to protect
him by fixing the prices he has to pay after
the manner that wages are now fixed.

Thus in Australia Protection has become, in a much fuller sense than it is in
any other country in the world, a national
policy. It is fixing itself like a million-
rooted parasite in every fibre of the national
life. Australia's economic policy is definite
and absolute—Protection of the Prohibition
genus. It goes as far beyond Canadian
Protection as Canadian Protection is beyond
Free Trade, and its kind of Protection is as
different from the Canadian Protection as two
policies called by the same name well can be.

There is in Australian politics, however, a small glimmer of a sentiment which
runs counter to its economic policy. The

Imperial sentiment leads a section—some of the followers of Mr. Deakin—to offer lip-service to Imperial preference, and we must consider whether this section is likely to secure any modification in the Protective programme.

On a cursory glance we are not encouraged, for the leaders of the group have owed, and still owe, all political influence they have to their alliance with the Labour Party, and the sole ground for this alliance is that they stand for the Protection of which the Labour Party is the chief champion.

If we study their speeches our suspicions as to their trade policy are placed beyond dispute. Mr. Deakin is a Protectionist, and has declared many times that Australian labour should supply Australian demands. His acting Home Secretary, Mr. Mauger, has attributed the difficulties of finding openings for apprentices to engineering in Australia to the importation of English machinery. He has attacked English boots, candles, clothing, and has demanded their practical exclusion. Every Minister in the present Australian Cabinet has spoken in the same strain.

When the Imperial Preferentialists

drafted a Bill to embody their ideas, its inadequacy was apparent to every one. It lowered no duties in favour of the British importer, and it gave him preference in respect to goods of which only £900,000 worth came from foreign countries. "The Ministry," said one of its critics in the Upper House, "had made an attempt to translate this cry of Preferential Trade into law. But the Bill which was introduced dealt with not more than one-twelfth of the total trade between Great Britain and Australia, and in no single case did it propose to lower the tariff in favour of Great Britain. It was not preferential admission but preferential exclusion. It was a preference of shams and delusions, embedded in humbug, so far as Great Britain was concerned."

New Zealand presents no special features. Mr. Seddon, in 1903, secured the passing of amendments to the Customs Act which had the effect of increasing the duties on certain articles when imported from foreign countries, but the tariff in favour of the New Zealand manufacturer was in every case left at a substantial height.[1]

[1] For instance, boots from England had still to bear 22½ per cent. ; furniture, 25 per cent. ; hardware, 20

South Africa has had little chance of showing its hand. It has been in a disorganised state since an Imperial Trade Policy has become a subject of serious discussion. But since the South African Customs Union Convention in 1903 goods of British manufacture have benefited by a rebate of 25 per cent., or where the customs duty was one of 2½ per cent. *ad valorem* they have been admitted free. See table on p. 89.

This survey of the Trade policy of the Imperial States enables us to come to certain conclusions which seem to be inevitable from the facts.

These Imperial States are busy building up native industries behind a protection wall, some being still in the "infant industry" stage of protection, others having advanced beyond it but having adopted a policy of "new protection" in order to enable them to keep up a high standard of working-class income.

Every one of the States, in respect to products which it is manufacturing or trying

per cent. ; earthenware, 20 per cent.; paper, 5s. per cwt. These duties make it perfectly obvious that New Zealand is also only to allow us to compete for the residue of New Zealand consumption.

The slight effect of these preferences is seen by the following table ; the war vitiates the Cape Colony figures.

	1900.	1901.	1902.	1903.	1904.	1905.
	£	£	£	£	£	£
NEW ZEALAND—						
From United Kingdom	6,504,484	6,885,831	6,851,452	7,512,668	7,982,340	7,795,284
From Foreign Countries	1,516,240	2,018,218	1,905,766	2,140,533	2,261,772	2,119,215
CAPE COLONY—						
From United Kingdom	13,018,953	14,198,748	22,304,990	21,703,663	14,028,922	12,386,880
From Foreign Countries	3,631,691	4,417,507	7,841,969	9,827,416	5,080,171	4,052,370
CANADA—						
From United Kingdom	9,203,369	8,839,349	10,114,579	12,106,585	12,698,724	12,403,779
From Foreign Countries	27,207,188	27,613,374	30,607,940	34,693,717	36,707,121	38,951,710

to manufacture, regards British imports with the same hostility as it regards imports from other countries, and when it allows a preference to Great Britain over foreign rivals it does so only after it has amply protected its own producers. Every State is determined to produce everything it can by its own manufacturers, so that the residue of the demand which the native manufacturers cannot supply, and for the supply of which Preferential tariff gives the British manufacturer an advantage over the foreign manufacturer, is not at all regarded as the permanent perquisite of the Imperial manufacturer, but is to be absorbed by the native protected factories at the earliest possible time. The Colony for the Colonists is the basis of its trade and tariff policies.

The Imperial Preference proposals therefore amount to this, that we are asked to permanently change our trade policy for certain small advantages of a temporary nature on the Colonial markets. Moreover, the effect of the agitation so far has been to lead the Colonies to assume that the Mother Country is in some way neglecting their interests. It has not shattered in the least the Colonial determination to

exclude everything—both foreign and British
—which they can manufacture themselves,
and it has put obstacles in the way of the
Colonies granting preference to the Mother
Country, as Canada has done, not for the
purpose of securing preference on the Home
market, but as some recognition of the Imperial bond and of the sacrifices which the
Mother Country has to make for Imperial
maintenance.

But there is a general argument which the
Tariff Imperialists use and which should be
noticed. It is asserted that all the great
European wars have been trade wars.
"How came we to conquer India?" asks
Sir John Seeley.[1] "Was it not a direct consequence of trading with India? And that
is only the most conspicuous illustration
of a law which prevails throughout English
history in the seventeenth and eighteenth
centuries, the law, namely, of the inter-
dependence of war and trade, so that
throughout that period trade leads naturally
to war and war fosters trade." From this
it is argued that just as trade rivalry has
pushed us into war, so, only by trade
union, or by an Imperial Zollverein, can
the Empire be kept united.

[1] "Expansion of England," pp. 109, 110.

During the controversy which culminated in the election of 1906 this claim in some of its aspects received a great deal of attention, and indeed was so thoroughly threshed out in these aspects that nothing new can be said. The honours of the contest appear to me to rest with those who argued that a trading bond is an irritating bond; that however much trading advantage may be an element in Imperial stability, the placing of such advantage in the forefront of the *raison d'être* of Empire makes the Imperial fabric a gross erection of the commercial spirit—a kind of United States sky-scraper valued because of its utility in raking in rents—and such erections do not stand the test of time.

But there is a reply to the Trade-foundation-of-Empire School which is more fundamental and fatal than the damaging examination in detail to which it has been subjected. This school has never appreciated the trade policy of the Colonies. It has not grasped the significance of Colonial protection. Australia is as determined to retain its own market as Germany is, and though the Australian tells you that it will be a long time before he will have surplus manufactured products to export, he is doing his best to hasten that time. Upon foreign markets Australia will compete with Great Britain in precisely the same spirit as America does. Now if Australia were willing to put itself in the position which Mr. Chamberlain foreshadowed in his Glasgow speech,[1] when he said that the Colonies would not seek to manufacture what we now send to them, provided we gave them a moderate preference on our markets, the Imperial trade school might well remind us of these European wars and warn us against allowing our Colonies to become separate fiscal entities. But they are separate fiscal entities. They have become separate national industrial units. In every competitive field where they appear, Britain, as much as Germany or America, is their enemy. "If we are to be killed," said an ex-President of the Canadian Manufacturers' Association, "it makes no difference to us whether it be by a Yankee or by a Britisher."

A reciprocity treaty with Germany or the United States is therefore just as likely to unite us and these countries in the bonds of

---

[1] October 6, 1903. His statement was modified when he published the speeches of his Fiscal campaign because he had come to see that the Colonies would never agree to it.

everlasting peace as Preferential Trade is likely to unite the Imperial States in an everlasting Imperial bond. If trade rivalry is bound to have the political influence which the Tariff Imperialists of the historical school claim for it, their arguments prove not the efficacy of Preferential Trade but its futility in view of the policy of industrial development and rivalry which the Imperial States have embarked upon. Preferential Trade would not diminish by one iota the trade rivalry which has already grown up between the Mother Country and the Imperial States. If the preference is sufficiently real to enable British goods to compete with Colonial goods on the Colonial market, the rivalry is more likely to be sharpened.

We must therefore make up our minds that the Imperial States are not to sacrifice a particle of their industrial interests for the sake of the Mother Land's trade. As they are Protectionist, I think we might reasonably expect them to give us preference over foreign producers who bear none of our Imperial responsibilities, and who in the event of war are more likely to be the enemies than the defenders of the Colonial peoples.

Even to such a policy strong economic

interests in the Colonies are opposed. There are, for instance, the manufacturers who use raw material, such as dyes. They would oppose any preference to the Imperial States on the ground that such preference would increase the Colonial cost of production—or they would assent to it only on the ground that they had higher Protection for their finished produce and so be able to increase prices to the Colonial consumer.

Free Trade within the Empire is not a practical policy as yet. In Canada the Free Trade movement is not losing ground although the industrial centres of Quebec and Ontario are Protectionist ; but, owing to the alliance between Labour legislation and Protection in Australasia, the Free Trade movement there has received a decided setback. The same is true of New Zealand, and South Africa will probably insist upon going through the weary process of Protection, more Protection, still more Protection.

For what advantages Imperial Trade brings to Imperial stability the Labour Party looks in a totally different direction from that of Conservative Imperialism. Imperial markets do not afford opportunities for sufficiently important negotiations. Low

Imperial postage rates, the same coinage, special facilities provided by the State for spreading commercial information, though savouring somewhat of the parish pump in contrast with the grandiose pageantry of the proposals for an Imperial Preference, are, nevertheless, more substantial and practical.

But what of the sea? Imperial trade suffers no more serious handicap than that imposed upon it by shipping rings and railway companies which exploit the Imperial needs of transport for their own purposes, which hamper the ready flow of Imperial trade, and, for an insignificant percentage, turn the British seaman off the waters in favour of the Lascar.

Here the Labour Parties of the Empire come in, and that of Australia has led the way. Already a Royal Commission appointed by the Commonwealth House of Representatives has considered the question, and has collected figures which are available for any Australian Government which desires to take action. On the other hand Mr. Sidney Buxton, by reducing the cost of postage on British magazines to Canada, will do more for genuine Imperialism than all the poems and speeches launched by perfervid poets and talkers upon the heads of the British public.

Preferential trade is the proposal of individual capitalists who desire to make profits out of our Imperial connections; the Imperial organisation of trade routes and facilities is the proposal of the Labour Party which desires the establishment of an efficient means for the exchange of material and intellectual productions throughout the Empire.

G

VI

THE DEPENDENCIES

IT is sometimes said that the more developed races have no right to demand an exchange of goods from the Tropics. I do not think that that view can be maintained. The Tropics can yield much to keep the Temperate lands in comfort and to sweeten life for them, and the Temperate lands have a right to ask from the Tropics some of their desirable productions. The world is the inheritance of all men. Tribes and nations have no right to peg off parts of the earth and separate them from the rest as much as though they had been withdrawn to the moon.

But this right of the Temperate Zone populations to enjoy the products of the Tropics does not override the superior right of the Tropical peoples to be treated as human beings. The white nations which exploit the Tropics economically assume responsibility for the natives, and how to fulfil that responsibility is the kernel of the problem of dependency government. This responsibility, however, may be regarded from a worthier point of view than as a consequent of economic exploitation. A community may well claim that it has a duty imposed upon it to spread the blessings of its civilisation over the earth. Morality has a universal sway, and by reason of its *imperium* the more developed nations are brought into a position of something like guardian and teacher of the less developed nations.

That is the theory. The danger is that the theory may be used to justify a totally inconsistent practice. National egotism rather than moral destiny may be the moving spring of the nation which brags about its "white man's burden," and as a matter of experience this high ethical justification has been more honoured by breach than by observance. Instead of the more developed nations having sent their educational and moral agents to aid the development of these backward peoples, they have sent their exploiters. They have begun by uprooting native civilisations, by destroying the economic expressions of these civilisations—such as tribal lands, by forcing the native mind into new grooves which that mind does not fit and never can fit. One hears the British official condemn the tribal system because it does not produce British virtues, and he points to native specimens of self-help and British individualism, who are tragic grotesques. One sees schools where native children are brought to be moulded into coloured Englishmen (I was present whilst some native children in a Fiji school were taught to march and drill to the tune of "Bonnie Dundee," the words of which they had committed to memory and were singing); one is brought to meetings where Hawaiians are taught all the iniquities of American political machine methods; one is shown barrack orphan asylums where kind women dote upon poor little coloured outcasts. It is hard to utter a critical word upon it all. Those responsible were so single-minded and so enthusiastic. But in spite of this lavishing of care, the native dies —dies of disease, we are told—dies because he cannot stand the physical infirmities of the white when they attack him. This, too, is a delusion. The disease that the white man has given to the black is fearful, but it does not explain the mysterious fading away of the native races. They seem to be bewitched when the white man comes. The failure is psychological. The native finds his old world to have vanished, and the new one is alien to him. He turns his face to the wall and dies. He does not understand the game. "Bonnie Dundee" rather than phthisis is his poison. In some places, with disgraceful ferocity, we have killed his body; in others, with the very loftiest intentions, we have killed his soul—and in both cases the results are the same. When he survives, he is not the old native. He is another being, without a past and without a future.

One of the most glaring faults of our Colonial Office is that it has no conscious concern in experimenting with native policies. We have the most magnificent opportunities for studying the conditions of native life, and the use we make of these opportunities is insignificant. Men like Sir Godfrey Lagden and Sir Marshal Clarke have contributed most admirable studies to the administration of natives, but they are sealed up in the dulness and irrelevancies of dust-laden blue-books. It is left to Chicago University to send a commissioner to study native administration, and to an American publisher to issue the results, whilst our Civil Service Commissioners set examination-papers with apparently the sole end in view of refraining to test the latent practical capacity of the men who are to be

responsible for our racial burdens. Any reform in our native administration must be
preceded by an alteration in our Civil Service
tests.   A reform in the Civil Service is essential to the democratisation of the Empire.

Our fundamental mistake in native policy
is that we regard the native as a Briton in
the making.   Even Radicals fall into that
error when they assume that the end of
our native administration must of necessity
be the self-government of the people.   The
development of their own organisation, not
the imposing of the ends of our national life,
should be the purpose of our government
of dependencies.   In some cases it ought
to be the re-establishment of the rule of the
chiefs ; in others, a restoration of a kind
of semi-democracy in which the people are
partly enfranchised or elect part of the
governing authority.   In every case the
native should be protected from the blight-
ing exploitation of white men's capitalism ;
obstacles should be placed in the way of,
rather than encouragement given to, the
break-up of his tribal economic system ; his
traditional methods of legal administration
should not be supplanted by ours which he
cannot be taught to respect and often not
even to understand ; even his catalogue of

crimes should not be made the same as ours because he cannot understand our notions of right and wrong ;[1] finally, the less we interfere with native administration the better. We require Residents more than Governors.

Such a change is essential to the continuance of democracy at home. For, so long as we regard the native as some one whom *we* must rule, we are attempting the palpable impossibility of ruling democratically at home and despotically abroad. The result will be that our own democracy will be tainted, and our democratic systems will crumble, eaten to the heart of their supports by the autocracy of our dependency rule. "Free nations cannot govern subject provinces."

Our great dependency, India, offers special problems of its own which cannot be adequately dealt with here. Its present condition is profoundly unsatisfactory. Its civilisation, unlike that of Fiji or Jamaica, is equal, if not superior, to our own. It contains races that have had a proud and a powerful past. Its acquisition was by a conquest of peoples who

[1] One of the most disquieting sights one can see whilst visiting our tropical dependencies is crowds of natives dressed in prison clothes wandering carelessly about the streets, running errands for officials, and apparently held in no disfavour by the freemen and quite innocent of any shame.

brought an organised resistance to bear
against us, and not by a diplomatic subjection
of primitive tribes. The Indian communities
have developed complex political forms and
have stubbornly resisted disintegration on
the one hand and assimilation on the other.
Therefore it is pre-eminently true as regards
India that our Government should win the
confidence and assent of the people.

But here again our fatal incapacity to put
ourselves in the position of a civilisation different from our own shows itself.   We have
impoverished India by blessing it with land
legislation which would be a boon to the
Scottish peasant; we have administered its
affairs as though it were an ancient English
city proud of official banquets and honoured
by special trains; we have put on our usual
airs and our little upstart officials carry into
its remotest corners British superiority and
create and uphold a system of social para-
sitism with all its attendant vices.   India is
pre-eminently the perquisite of the classes.
They rule it; they exploit it.

Its problem is very complicated.   In the
first place it is not a national but a geographical expression.   It cannot be ruled from
one centre.   Even under the most extreme
form of democracy it must be a federation of

practically independent States, and, whether we like it or not, we cannot refuse to admit that the differences which keep its races apart are so acute that some over-authority will always be necessary to secure religious and civil liberty and peace.

The immediate reforms necessary are a lightening of India's financial load by relieving it of the Imperial burdens which it now unjustly bears, and a readjustment of taxes; the extension of local and State self-government, and further opportunities for natives to be employed in public offices; the freeing of the Press. The tide of reforming anxiety has receded far since Lord Ripon's day, and upon the bare sands Mr. Kipling and his kind have pitched their tents. They have entertained us with their art, and they have flattered us with their panegyrics. But India still lies an unsolved problem. If our Imperialist trumpeters have deafened our ears, India's voice has nevertheless not been stilled. The strident assertion of the magnificence of the British political genius has allayed no pangs of famine and soothed no grievances.

Hitherto our dependency rule has had the levelling effect of a steam-roller rather than the vitalising effect of a fresh breeze.

CONCLUSION

WE live at a time when the Fates are busy nurturing Destiny. But the life which is below appears but confusedly at the surface, and we dispute and get angry with each other as to its meaning.

We are certain that old political faiths no longer give us safe guidance; that the shibboleths of half a century ago are no longer the open-sesame to political wisdom. We are in another epoch of thought. The principles of Conservatism as we once heard them preached, equally with the principles of Democracy as we once heard them professed, are now relics of a generation that has passed and has left its dwelling-places in ruin and decay.

From this paralysis of age and confusion of birth a new party has arisen with a new gospel. Like all parties that grow from the bosom of nature and in the fulness of time— and that are, in consequence, to last—the Labour Party appears to some to be but

an old party, and its principles as ancient
as the hills. In a sense that is correct.
But newness in Party politics does not depend upon discoveries of new proposals but
in co-ordinating into a system of thought
old experiments, in making the rule what
have hitherto been exceptions, and our guides
and philosophers what have hitherto been
casual wayside acquaintances, in revivify-
ing old principles by bringing them afresh
into touch with life.

This is what the Labour Party has done.
From a fresh point of view—that of the man
who labours for a living—it is approaching
questions of religion, art, politics, administration, and it is hammering out the principles and expressions of an industrial state.
It has not been born in one country; it has
appeared in all. It is therefore not the product of national circumstances, but of the
stage of civilisation which the world has
now reached. It expresses needs which
are pressing themselves upon the attention
of every industrial country under heaven.
In this respect it is like the Liberal epoch
which died away in the strife of Nationalist
exclusiveness and jealousy that has dominated western policy for the last forty years.

Liberalism with its political democracy, economic free trade, religious toleration was a world movement—the movement of the liberated intellect ; Socialism (the inspiring principle of all Labour Parties whether they know it or not) is the next world movement —the movement of the constructive intellect. Being historical, it does not quarrel with historical facts. It contents itself with explaining them, and with apportioning blame and praise amongst the people who moulded them ; but it does not seek to go back upon them when once they have passed beyond the stage of contemporary change—when once systems of government and of thought have adjusted themselves to the events. The Labour Party therefore no more thinks of discussing whether the Stuarts should be restored to the throne than it does of debating whether we should break the Empire to pieces. But it approaches Imperial problems with the politics of the industrious classes as guide on the one hand, and the internationalism of its nature as guide on the other. If it feels the pride of race, it understands that other peoples can respond to the same thrill. Its Imperialism is therefore not of the aggressive or the bragging order ; it does not believe in the subjection of other nationalities ; it takes no pride in the government of " other " peoples. To its subject races it desires to occupy the position of friend ; to its self-governing Imperial States it seeks to be an equal; to the world it asks to be regarded as a neighbour.

For some years the thought of force has dominated national policies. Europe, weary of the strain of steering steadily towards justice and frightened by the threatening things which lie upon such a course, has frankly lapsed into the mood of militarism, of tariffs, of suspicion. And yet there is not a country in all the West but would escape with gladness from its awful imprisonment in the frowning fortresses of aggressive nationalism to which a resort to force always dooms a people. The spell is to be broken only by one of the nations boldly walking out from the imprisonment. What nation is more fitted to do that than we are ?

After a lapse of years, the Labour Movement in England stands once more in the forefront of the Labour movement of the world. Wherever Parliament is supreme and political Democracy established, the tactics and the principles of our Independent

Labour Party are being adopted, and a new friendship has sprung up between us and the Continental working-class movement. Who is to measure the opportunities which the British Labour Party now has, if it has the courage to put its hand to the great and difficult work which invites its energies ? It is not a Factory Act, or Trade Unionist Party. It is a Party in British politics, and its interests are as wide as British interests, and its aims are nothing narrower or meaner than the ends of British development. In every one of our Imperial States it has its kindred Parties—indeed in Australia, the Labour Parties are either in office or are the second largest Party in the State. Perhaps their isolation from the rest of the world has made them a little parochial, and they, least of all the Labour movements, reflect the characteristic spirit of internationalism.

But even now, before the Australian Labour Parties have been brought into very close contact with the European Labour movement, one can observe a striking difference between the attitude of these Parties to us at home and that which the other Colonial Parties bear to their home counterparts.

The nationalism of the Labour Party is mainly industrial. When it cries "Australia for the Australians" it means Australian work for Australian workmen, not a system of parochial politics. It distrusts Downing Street as much as any Party does, but it does not find it impossible to conceive of an Imperial alliance. It is jealous to guard the self-government of Australia, but it has not the petty spirit of nationalism which is one of the few unpleasant features of Australian life. The Labour Party more than any other Australian Party is possessed of the spirit which would allow it to take an organic place in a self-governing Empire with Imperial standards of administration to which local policies would conform.

In Canada, New Zealand, South Africa, Labour Parties grow. Their economic problems are the same as ours; their fundamental political aims are the same as ours; their democracy is of the same species as ours. They have no interest in a class dominance of the Empire; the South African War and its sequel have taught them much and have drawn them closer than ever they were to our movement here;

they have no confidence in Conservative rule at home; we are their allies; we and they together must build up an Imperial policy if that policy is to be democratic. We have been kept apart because intercommunication was difficult and was in hostile hands. As yet it must be admitted, when we approach Colonial problems we do so from unfamiliar points of view; when they approach ours they are also strangers to the considerations that weigh with us. But the fundamental similarity of the aims and methods of the Parties must speedily tell and produce an understanding between them. Then will begin a new chapter in the story of our Empire.

THE END

Printed by BALLANTYNE, HANSON & Co.
Edinburgh & London

THE LABOUR IDEAL

THE SOCIALIST'S BUDGET

THE SOCIALIST'S BUDGET

BY

PHILIP SNOWDEN, M.P.

LONDON: GEORGE ALLEN
156, CHARING CROSS ROAD
1907

Printed by BALLANTYNE, HANSON & Co.
At the Ballantyne Press, Edinburgh

Publisher's Note

Socialism being one of the most important subjects of to-day, its opponents and supporters alike need a frank, precise, and absolutely authentic account of its aim and methods. The Publisher wishes by means of this series to put clearly before the public a complete conspectus of the present policy of the English Socialists and the Independent Labour Party. To ensure authority and precision, arrangements have been made with the acknowledged leaders, in action and thought, of the new movement to contribute volumes to the " Labour Ideal" series on those branches of Socialism with which they are particularly connected.

The Publisher does not, of course, hold himself responsible for the opinions of the writers.

CONTENTS

CHAP.   PAGE

   I. A SOCIALIST CANON OF TAXATION   .   I

  II. THE SOCIAL INIQUITY OF RICHES   .   9

 III. THE WRONG OF INDIRECT TAXATION . 13

 IV. HOW THE POOR ARE TAXED   .   . 21

  V. SOURCES OF DIRECT TAXATION .   . 32

 VI. INCOME TAX REFORMS 40

VII. THE DISTRIBUTION OF WEALTH . . 46

VIII. FISCAL AND OTHER REFORMS   .   . 56

 IX. OLD AGE PENSIONS   .   .   . 65

  X. FINDING THE MILLIONS   .   . 73

 XI. THE DEATH DUTIES   .   .   . 80

XII. THE SOCIALIST'S BUDGET   .   . 86

THE SOCIALIST'S BUDGET

CHAPTER I

A SOCIALIST CANON OF TAXATION

SOCIALISTS look to the Budget as a means not only of raising revenue to meet unavoidable expenditure, but as an instrument for redressing inequalities in the distribution of wealth.

An increase in national taxation has no terrors for the Socialist, provided that the revenue be wisely and economically administered, and that the incidence of the taxation be just.

Socialists aim at the transfer to public ownership and control of such industrial concerns as can be managed better by the Municipality or the State. They maintain that experience justifies the claim that public management is more efficient and more economical than private control.

A

The private ownership of Land and Industrial Capital enables the proprietary classes to take in the form of Rent, Interest, and Profit enormous sums for permission to use the earth and the industrial machinery of the country. The purpose of Socialism is to transfer Land and Industrial Capital to the people. There are two ways in which, simultaneously, this object may be carried out.

The one way is, by the municipal and national appropriation (with such compensation to the existing owners as the community may think fit to give) of the land and industrial concerns. To the extent to which public ownership of land and capital exists will the private appropriation of rent and profit be stopped and money be available for purposes of public utility.

The second method is by Taxation. Taxation has its special sphere of usefulness in helping the community to secure some part of its own, by diverting into the national purse portions of the Rent, Interest, and Profit which now go to keep an idle class in luxury at the expense of the industrious poor.

It is with the possibilities and the ways of using taxation to advance Socialist aims and to finance schemes of social reform that I am in this essay concerned.

Startling as the cold-blooded declaration of the Socialist aim, and of the Socialist designs on taxation, may sound to those to whom they are unfamiliar, there is really nothing new suggested either in the principle or in the practice. There is no limit to the present rating powers of the local authority, nor to the taxing powers of the State. Each authority can compel the ratepayers or the tax-payers to contribute to the extent of the requirements of the locality or of the nation.

An interesting fact showing the antiquity of this public claim on private property is furnished by an Act of Parliament passed in the reign of Charles II., under which the Overseers of the Poor may raise by taxation money to buy "stock of wares and stuff with which to set the poor on work, to relieve the poor and to apprentice the children, taxation being according to ability, it having been held that the inhabitants of parishes, townships, and villages are liable in respect of their ability derived from the profits of stock-in-trade and of other property, to be taxed."

There have been times of distress when the demands of the Poor Law have exacted a local rate of over twenty shillings in the pound.

The recognised limits to local and national taxation are the needs of the respective authorities. Though not perhaps clearly or generally understood, the taxing powers of the community are based upon the principle that private property is only permitted to be held or enjoyed by individuals so long as that private possession is not opposed to the general welfare, and so long as the community does not require the property or the income for public purposes. The principle is well known in law, and constantly acted upon, that public needs and the public safety are superior to individual claims, and that the latter may be called upon to be sacrificed to their utmost limit to meet the higher necessities of the community.

Illustrations of the foregoing principle applied are to be seen on every hand. The State acquisition of the Telegraphs and the Telephones, and the municipalisation of gas and of water supplies and of tramway services are cases in point. The Land Clauses Act entitles the community to expropriate the private possessors of land and property by giving such compensation as the community may regard as just.

The whole history of municipal rating and of national taxation, especially during the last twenty or thirty years, is the record of the extension of the principle that Rent, Interest, and Profit must be devoted to public purposes just as public needs mature. Neither can it be argued that the increased taxation of property and income has been imposed only to pay for the increased benefit which the class taxed has received or been able to enjoy under the protection of the State. As a matter of fact, the receivers of Rent, Interest, and Profit have, concurrently with increased local and national taxation, taken yearly increasing sums, but that is because by the power of their monopoly they have been able to take advantage of the yearly increase of wealth production. Local rates and national taxes have not been raised deliberately because the capacity of the propertied class to pay more has grown, but

because the needs of the municipality and
of the State have become greater. The
increased amount which the community
has appropriated by the heavier rating
and taxation of the receivers of Rent,
Interest, and Profit has been imposed
regardless of the greater capacity of this
class to pay. The point we wish to enforce
is that the propertied tax-payers are paying
increased taxation, not because they have
been growing richer so rapidly, but because
increased taxation was required, and the
State exercised its power to tax individuals
according to their ability to pay.

The Socialist accepts the principle of
taxation—taxation "according to ability
derived from the profits of stock-in-trade
and other property," but desires deliberately
to incorporate another idea and purpose
in taxation, namely, the taxation of the
rich to secure such socially-created wealth
as is now taken in Rent, Interest, and
Profit, and to use this revenue for social
reform purposes. In other words, we would
by that means compel "the rendering unto
Cæsar the things that are Cæsar's."

Though the liability of property to practically unlimited taxation is recognised in

law and in practice, it is true, too, that taxation is levied with the idea of securing from every citizen a contribution to the State in proportion to the benefit he is supposed to derive from the protection of the State.

The Socialist subscribes to the doctrine that each individual ought to contribute to the support of the State in proportion to the benefit he derives from the State, but he would maintain stoutly that the incidence of present taxation does not fulfil this requirement. The rich do not contribute in proportion to the benefits they receive or to their ability to pay, whilst the poor are taxed out of all proportion to the return they get or to their power to contribute. The proof of this may be postponed to a later chapter.

The Socialist's ideas of taxation may be briefly summarised as follows :—

1. Both local and national taxation should aim, primarily, at securing for the communal benefit all "unearned" or "social" increment of wealth.

2. Taxation should aim, deliberately, at preventing the retention of large incomes and great fortunes in private hands, recognising

that the few cannot be rich without making the many poor.

3. Taxation should be in proportion to ability to pay and to protection and benefit conferred by the State.

4. No taxation should be imposed which encroaches upon the individual's means to satisfy his physical needs.

CHAPTER II

THE SOCIAL INIQUITY OF RICHES

THE taxation of the rich to raise the standard of life of the masses can be justified on many grounds. "There is no wealth but Life," says John Ruskin. "That country is the richest which nourishes the greatest number of noble and happy human beings." The test of civilisation is in the extent to which the people as a whole enjoy the blessings of rational progress. One millionaire is no social compensation for one hundred thousand paupers. In the moral and well-ordered State it will be the aim to secure a moderate degree of comfort for all rather than to encourage one to get the command of luxury by depriving others of the means of obtaining necessaries.

The Socialist believes that the existence of a rich class is a danger to the State. He cordially endorses the conclusions of Professor Cairnes, who writes: "That useful function which some profound writers fancy they discover in the abundant expenditure of the idle rich turns out to be a sheer illusion. Political Economy furnishes no such palliation of unmitigated selfishness. I think it is important, on moral no less than on economic grounds, to insist upon this, that no public benefit of any kind arises from the existence of an idle, rich class. The wealth accumulated by their ancestors and others on their behalf, where it is employed as capital, no doubt helps to sustain industry; but what they consume in luxury and idleness is not capital, and helps to sustain nothing but their unprofitable lives. By all means they must have their rent and interest as it is written in the bond, but let them take their place as drones in the hive, gorging at a feast to which they have contributed nothing."

Professor Cairnes insists that it should be recognised on moral grounds that no public advantage comes from the existence of an idle, rich class. The Socialist goes farther than that, and insists that such a class is an iniquity, and that the interests of social well-being demand that the drones be driven from the social hive, or that they be deprived of their means to live in idleness and luxury, whilst those who make the wealth they spend are hungry, naked, and cold.

The existence of a rich class, whose riches are the cause of the poverty of the masses, is the justification for the Socialist demand that the cost of bettering the condition of the people must be met by the taxation of the rich. But there is the additional practical reason that urgent social reform cannot be carried out by any other means.

The Chancellor of the Exchequer admits the urgency of Old Age Pensions, but confesses his inability to find the money. The Prime Minister declares that there is no hope of carrying out the paltry reforms of Payment of Members and Payment of Election Expenses until there has been retrenchment of national expenditure. To these wise men has not yet come the revelation of the only way and means.

Old Age Pensions is a proposal to which every political party in the State is committed. To admit the need of State Old Age Pensions is to confess that the working classes are too poor to provide for their own old age. If it be so, they are too poor to be taxed for Old Age Pensions. The cost, therefore, if it is to come, must come from the incomes of the rich. If the masses are to be taxed to meet the cost of State schemes intended for their benefit, then no benefit will come to them. It will not be social reform unless it adds to the workers' command of necessaries and comforts. To tax the class which needs Old Age Pensions would simply result in the reduction of the necessary expenditure of that class in some other direction.

On the grounds of morality, justice, and necessity, the taxation of the rich for social reform purposes is justifiable.

CHAPTER III

PARTY and class interests have a great deal more to do with fixing the incidence of taxation than has any theory of just taxation, or any desire to conform to Adam Smith's canons of taxation.

A Chancellor of the Exchequer has always to shape the Budget so as to arouse the least measure of opposition amongst those who are the most influential supporters of his Party. The propertied classes have been the people who have controlled Parliament hitherto. At present there are evidences that the working people are beginning to see the importance of being directly represented in Parliament, and of having legislation considered from their point of view. In the past, the workers have either not been represented at all, or they have quietly submitted to be led to political slaughter by the landlords, the lawyers, and the capitalists.   The result has been that the propertied classes have evaded taxing themselves as far as possible, and have made the burden of taxation on the poor as heavy as their bent backs were able to carry.

The taxation of the poor has been imposed, deliberately, in such a way as to make it difficult for the poor to understand that they were taxed so heavily.   A Parliament of rich men has known far better than to attempt to impose direct taxation upon the masses.   The great William Pitt, in the course of a debate on a proposal to levy a direct income-tax upon all citizens, put the danger of such a proposal in very telling language: "A direct tax of 7 per cent.," said he, "would cause a bloody revolution.   There is a far better way than that, a way in which you can tax the last rag from the back and the last bite from the mouth without ever hearing a murmur about heavy taxation.   And it is by taxing a large number of articles in daily use. The tax will then be lost in the price of the article.   The people will grumble about high prices and hard times, but they will never know that the hard times are caused by heavy taxation."

This has been the principle upon which Governments have acted in the past—to tax the people to the utmost limit by indirect taxation, and to tax their own class only when the working class could bear no more, and additional revenue had to be raised. It is still openly admitted by Chancellors of the Exchequer that they regard the Income Tax as, not a permanent, but a temporary expedient, to be available only as a supplement to other forms of taxation, chiefly indirect.

Indirect taxation has nothing whatever to recommend it to an intelligent people, however advantageous it may be to the well-to-do. Indirect taxation violates every principle of sound economy. It does not tax a person according to his ability, but according to his necessities. It compels the payment of the tax at a time inconvenient to the tax-payer. It takes out of the pocket of the tax-payer much more than it brings into the treasury of the State. It is uncertain in its incidence, and open to evasion. It taxes one individual of the same class more heavily than another. It does not encourage a critical supervision of taxation amongst those who pay the taxes. For these and other reasons, indirect taxation, though maintained, is not defended as just or economical by politician or economist. Its maintenance is excused on the ground that indirect taxation is the only means by which the working class can be made to contribute to the cost of national government at all.

But there are two or three reasons, each one by itself sufficient, why the poorer working classes should not be taxed by the Government at all. The first reason is that the workers pay the taxes which are levied upon the idle rich. The person who does no work is living upon those who do, be he unemployed labourer or unemployed millionaire. The workers, therefore, pay the bulk of the taxation taken in the form of income tax and death duties. The idle rich get the full protection of Government, and others pay for it ; and the majority of those who pay for this State protection of the enjoyments of the rich have neither property, employment, nor sustenance guaranteed to them by the State.

If it be admitted that taxation should be in proportion to protection and benefit received from the State, and in proportion to ability to pay, the taxation of the working classes must be acknowledged to be unjust. With 43 per cent. of the working classes living in poverty, with an average wage over the whole working class not sufficient to provide themselves with the standard of workhouse comfort, it becomes a crime to tax them for the protection of their property and the enjoyment of their privileges.

In the rudest condition of human existence, without State, law, or taxes, the individual can provide himself with his creature needs. He can suffer privation only from the failure of Nature. He is never obliged to remain idle and starve while the State protects others in the possession of enormous wealth which he has helped to create, and which is mockingly expended in scandalous luxury.

The State can have no right to tax an individual until it has provided the conditions in which every willing worker is guaranteed the means of a healthy human life in return for useful work. The taxation of the necessaries of life in the existing state of things is an aggravation of the poverty of the people. Such taxation, in the words of Mr. Gladstone, "is in no small degree a deduction from a scanty store which is necessary to secure them a sufficiency not of the comforts of life, but even of the prime necessaries, of clothing, shelter, and of fuel." To tax poverty, and thereby deprive human beings of necessaries, whilst the rich have abundant stores, under the plea that all ought to contribute to the State, is an unjust and inhuman proceeding.

But waiving for the moment the contention in the preceding paragraphs, and granting the claim that all should contribute in proportion to their incomes, the over-taxation of the poor stands out as a shameful injustice. The larger part of the national revenue is raised from indirect taxation. Twelve shillings out of every pound comes from such a source. It is true that the disparity between the proportions has been growing less during the last ten years, owing to the increase in the death duties and the income tax. The proportion of the total of indirect taxation to the whole amount of taxation is less, but the actual sum paid in indirect taxation is very considerably greater. In 1899 the total Customs and Excise Revenue was £50,050,000. In 1905–6 the amount derived from these two departments was £70,229,000, an increase in seven years of

over £20,000,000, or 40 per cent. This
increase in working class taxation has been
contemporary with a general decline in the
wages of the workers.

Though there has been during the same
period an increase of direct taxation (income
tax, &c.) of £20,000,000, there has been
at the same time a continuous and considerable increase in the incomes of this class ;
that is, in the ability of the class liable to
taxation of that character. These two facts
prove that the burden of the recent increases
of taxation is being borne by the working
people.

The sum raised by Indirect Taxation in
the year 1905–6 was £70,229,000, made up
as follows :—

CUSTOMS RECEIPTS

Coal Tax	£2,184,000
Cocoa	273,000
Chicory and Coffee . .	230,000
Dried Fruits . . .	475,000
Foreign Spirits . . .	3,894,000
Sugar	6,178,000
Tea	6,815,000
Tobacco	13,381,000
Wine	1,176,000
Other articles . . .	49,000
Total Customs Receipts .	£34,655,000

EXCISE RECEIPTS

Spirits	£17,765,000
Beer	12,983,000
Glucose and Saccharine .	103,000
Railway Duty . . .	353,000
Licences	4,365,000
Other items	5,000
Total Excise Receipts .	£35,574,000
Total of Indirect Taxation	£70,229,000

To the above items of Indirect Taxation there might reasonably be added a sum of nearly £5,000,000 a year profit from the Post Office, and a sum of £8,153,000 from Stamps, both items being in reality forms of Indirect Taxation. If these two sums be added to the tables given above, the total receipts from Indirect Taxation amount to £83,316,500 out of a total revenue from taxes of £134,565,500; that is, about 62 per cent. of revenue is from Indirect Taxation.

CHAPTER IV

HOW THE POOR ARE TAXED

IT is, of course, impossible to ascertain exactly what proportion of the strictly Indirect Taxation is paid by the wage-earning classes, but it is beyond question that they contribute the great bulk of it. The articles of consumption and of ordinary use which are taxed are tea, coffee, chicory, beer, chloroform, cocoa, collodion, ether, dried fruits, glucose, molasses, soap (in which spirit has been used), spirits, sugar, sweetened milk, tobacco, wine, playing-cards.

The principal items of Indirect Taxation are the duties upon spirits, beer, sugar, tea, and tobacco. These four items are responsible for over £60,000,000 of revenue. Experts assign the proportion of the total annual Drink Bill of the United Kingdom contributed by the wage-earning classes at £100,000,000. Assuming this figure as the basis, we may get an approximate idea of the amount contributed by the working classes to the national revenue through the liquor taxes. A Committee of the British Association, reporting on the "Appropriation of Wages" in 1882, said that 75 per cent. of the total consumption of beer and spirits and 10 per cent. of the Wine Bill might be assigned as the shares of the working class. This basis works out that £26,500,000 of the revenue from drink taxes is contributed by the working classes.

The two other items which contribute largely to the revenue from Indirect Taxation are the Tea Duty and the Sugar Tax. It is indisputable that the working classes consume more tea per head than the wealthier classes. The average annual consumption of tea, according to the Customs Authorities, is 6 lbs. per head of the population. The average working-class family will, therefore, consume from 30 to 40 lbs. of tea a year, paying a duty of from 15s. to 20s. in 1905-6. Roughly, we may get at the amount of taxation upon tea, sugar, coffee, cocoa, fruit, and tobacco, contributed by the wage-earning classes, by assigning to them four-fifths of the total taxation

from these sources.   This will work out as
follows :—

Four-fifths of Tea Duty . .	£5,452,000
Four-fifths of Sugar Tax . .	4,940,000
Four-fifths of Tobacco Duty .	10,170,000
Four-fifths of Taxes from Coffee, Cocoa, Chicory, Dried Fruits	725,000
Total . . .	£21,287,000
Add working class Drink Taxation	26,500,000
Total working class contribution to Indirect Taxation . .	£47,787,000

The proportion of four-fifths as the working class portion of the whole community is
well within the mark if we take the working class as including families with a total
income of less than £160 a year.   Mr.
Chiozza Money, M.P., comes to the conclusion that such families comprise nine-
tenths of the total population.   It should be
borne in mind, however, that not far short
of one-half of this class of families have incomes so small that, if every penny be spent
on absolute necessaries, these are not enough
to provide a sufficiency of food, clothing,
and shelter.

The consumption of the articles enumerated in the above statement of Indirect
Taxation will be fairly uniform over the

whole of the families included among the working classes. The proportion of taxation to income, therefore, will rise with the poverty of the people. The average burden per head of the wage-earning classes laid by Indirect Taxation is £1, 7s. 6d. a year, or £6, 17s. 6d. per family of five persons.

The following extract from Mr. Seebohm Rowntree's book on "Poverty" will help to give an idea of the extent of working class poverty, and from it may be deduced some conclusions as to the severity and unjust proportion of taxation upon the very poor :—

CLASSIFICATION OF THE POPULATION OF YORK

Class.	Family Income (Average Family, i.e. Parents and two to four Children).	Number of Persons in each Class.	Percentage of each Class upon the total Wage Earners in York.	Average Earnings per Family.
	Per week.		Per cent.	
A	Under 18s. . . .	1,957	4.2	8s. 4½d.
B	18s. and under 21s.	4,492	9.6	19s. 9d.
C	21s. and under 30s.	15,710	33.6	26s. 7d.
D	Over 30s.	24,595	52.6	41s. 9¼d.
E	Female Domestic Servants . . .	4,296	...	...
F	Servant - keeping Class	21,830	...	...
G	In Public Institutions	2,932	...	...
		75,812	100	...

Taking £70 a year as representing the family income of a considerable portion of the working class, we shall arrive at the conclusion that this part of the population, though fighting a perpetual battle with want, pays an average of £6, 17s. 6d. per family in Indirect Taxation for national purposes, or a sum equal to an income tax of nearly 2s. in the pound. The well-to-do family of equal number, with an income of, say, £2000 a year, will not consume more taxable articles; their food, to a far greater extent, will consist of meat, milk, fruits, and other non-taxed articles. The amount of Indirect Taxation paid by two families of equal size, one with an income of £70, and the other £2000 a year, works out at 2s. in the pound on his income for the poor man, and for the rich man at just over ¾d. in the pound on his income. In proportion to his ability to pay, the poor man is taxed, indirectly, thirty times more than the rich man.

But this way of looking at the question does not show the whole of the wrong done to the poor by Indirect Taxation. Not only does the poor person pay enormously more in proportion to his ability to pay, but he actually pays more in taxation for an equal weight of the taxed commodity than does the rich man.

The poor man drinks cheap whisky and cheap tea, smokes cheap tobacco, and eats cheap sugar and cheap dried fruits. The tax is the same upon the cheap as upon the more expensive articles. Take tea and tobacco as illustrations of how this works out to the disadvantage of the poor. The average value of imported tea during 1904–5 was 7¼d. per lb. During this time the duty was 8d. and 6d. per lb. The tea almost universally bought by the working classes is retailed at 1s. 4d. per lb., including duty. The well-to-do pay up to 2s. 4d. a lb. With the duty at 6d. the poor pay a tea duty of 75 per cent. on the value of the tea; the rich are taxed but 27 per cent. upon the price they pay for their tea.

The same consideration for the pocket of the rich man is shown by a comparison of the duties on whisky and wine. The poor man's spirit is taxed 11s. 4d. a gallon, the rich man's champagne 2s. 6d. per gallon. The case of tobacco is more strikingly unjust. The duties upon tobacco are as follows :—

Manufactured cigars	.	.	6s. od. per lb.
Cavendish or Negrohead	.	4s. 4d. ,, ,,
Other tobacco	.	.	3s. 1od. ,, ,,

These duties are charged by weight, so that the common cigars and common tobacco (the poor man's penny cigar and his twist or shag) pay as much duty as the rich man's expensive smokes, ounce for ounce.   Out of every threepence the working man pays for tobacco, twopence-halfpenny is tax.   The poor man has a tax of 500 per cent. put upon the value of his tobacco.   The rich man who smokes shilling cigars pays only from 20 to 100 per cent. taxation.

Indirect taxation takes more from the poor, over and above what goes to the revenue, than it does in the case of the rich. As Customs Duties are paid when the goods leave bond, the trade profit is added to the tax as well as to the value of the goods, and the higher the proportion of the tax to the cost price, the larger becomes the trader's profit on the duty.

All proposals to remedy the glaring injustice of the taxation at the same rate without regard to the value of the article have been rejected by the Revenue Authorities as impracticable.   It is probably true that the difficulties of graduating a Customs Duty according to the value of the commodity are insuperable ; but be that as it may, the

injustice remains, and that fact is the reason
why taxes should not be imposed which
cannot be levied so as to bear evenly upon
all classes. And above all is the tax condemned when it must, from its character,
press more heavily upon the poor than
upon the rich.

It may be urged that some of the Indirect Taxation paid by the working classes
is self-imposed, or that, at least, they are
under no compulsion to pay it. It is true
that no person is compelled to drink beer or
spirits, to smoke tobacco, to eat sugar or
currants, or to drink tea and coffee. But
this sort of argument misses the very reason
why taxes are laid upon the articles mentioned. It is precisely because drink, tobacco,
tea, and sugar are so largely and so generally consumed that these articles are taxed.
The excuse given for the re-imposition of
the Sugar Tax and the Bread Tax during
the war was that it was desired to broaden
the basis of taxation. If the people gave up
drinking liquor and smoking tobacco, the
orthodox ideas of taxation would be the
cause of the immediate transfer of the taxes,
to some other articles which the people generally used or consumed.

Another very strong objection to Indirect Taxation is that already hinted at, namely, that the tax-payer has little knowledge of what he actually does pay in taxation. How many smokers, for instance, know that when they pay 3d. for an ounce of tobacco, only ½d. is for the tobacco and 2½d. for the tax. How many housewives know that there is a tax at all upon coffee, cocoa, rasins, or even upon sugar. When we remember the violent and successful opposition of the smokers to an increase of a halfpenny an ounce in the price of tobacco, some seven years ago, when the tobacco duty was increased, one may form some idea of the revolution which would come if the attempt were to be made now, for the first time, to put a 2½d. tax upon a halfpenny-worth of tobacco.

Indirect Taxation never brings home to a nation the price of its folly. The South African War, as everybody knows, cost £250,000,000; but by adding half the cost to the National Debt and one-half of the remainder to Indirect Taxation, the people have been prevented from fully appreciating the cost of the war, though paying it none the less, and suffering from it none the less.

If, instead of paying for this war by

Indirect Taxation largely, each family in the country had been served with a tax-demand for £30 (the average cost per family), it is certain the country would have turned and rent the Government responsible for this war, and this generation, at least, would have known war no more.

The National Debt is a colossal instance of the way in which Indirect Taxation has been used to blind the people to the folly and the cost of Empire and Glory. The National Debt to-day stands at just under £800,000,000, just about the figure at which it stood at the time of the Crimean War. During the nineteenth century the amount of interest paid upon the National Debt was £2,800,000,000 (two thousand eight hundred millions). Each generation has paid by taxation a sum equal to the amount of the debt. And notwithstanding, the debt still remains as large, practically, as ever, and this generation pays, without knowing it, £28,000,000 a year of taxation upon a war-debt incurred a hundred years ago.

Besides the Indirect Taxation upon the articles before mentioned, there are a number of other taxes taking the form of stamp duties and licences which come under the head of Indirect Taxation. Many of these taxes are small in amount, and cause an inconvenience and irritation altogether out of proportion to the revenue they contribute. Stamps upon receipts and agreements are a tax upon industry, and the licences for certain trades, such as house-agents, auctioneers, hawkers, pedlars, pawnbrokers, refreshment - house keepers, hackney carriages, tobacco dealers, plate dealers, game dealers, are survivals of a now undefended system of taxation, and act in the doubly injurious way of protecting certain trades and of imposing Indirect Taxation with all its bad effects, and without even the compensation of a revenue worth the trouble of collecting.

Under a just system of taxation all Indirect Taxation for revenue purposes would be abolished. Indirect Taxation, as we have seen, violates every accepted canon of just and equitable taxation. It is condemned by all economists. It is not defended by any political party out of office. Its abolition has been the election cry of the Radical Party for half a century. Indirect Taxation for revenue would find no place in the Socialist Budget.

CHAPTER V

SOURCES OF DIRECT TAXATION

THE revenue from Direct Taxation in
1905–6 was made up as follows:—

Estate Duty	£13,585,783
Probate Duty . . .	78,258
Account Duty . . .	3,146
Temporary Estate Duty .	10,117
Legacy Duty . . .	3,084,605
Succession Duty . . .	677,883
Corporation Duty . . .	48,344
Land Tax	720,000
House Duty	1,950,000
Property and Income Tax .	31,350,000
Total Direct Taxation .	£51,508,136

The objections to which Indirect Taxation
is open do not apply to the taxes enumerated
above, though the manner in which some of
these taxes are levied falls far short of an
ideal plan of taxation.

The Land Tax, which brought in last
year a sum of £720,000, is the survival of
a scheme enacted in 1692, whereby "every

person, body politic, and corporate, having
any estate in ready monies or in any debts
owing to them, or having any estate in
goods, wares, merchandise or other chattels
or personal estate whatsoever, within this
realm or without, shall yield and pay unto
their Majesties four shillings in the pound,
according to the true yearly value thereof."
A further section of the Act imposes a
tax of four shillings in the pound upon
all incomes from office or employment
for profit. The fourth section of the Act
expressly enacts a Land Tax "of four
shillings of every twenty shillings of the true
yearly value of all manors, messuages, lands
and tenements ; and quarries, mines, tithes,
tolls and all hereditaments whatsoever."

From 1692 to 1798 this Land Tax was
continued, the rate varying from one shilling
to four shillings in the pound, according to
the requirements of the Government. In
1798, however, the Land Tax was made
permanent, and fixed at four shillings in
the pound on the valuation of 1692, on all
rents and profits from real property. The
proportion due from each Parish was fixed,
and the precise amount is still levied on
every Parish in Great Britain, except where

the tax has been redeemed. The tax, when
first fixed in 1798, raised £1,905,077, but the
redemptions have brought down the revenue
from that figure to £720,000.

The increase in land values has reduced
the rate in the pound upon the present
rental to an insignificant sum in many parts
of the country, the rate in Lancashire amounting to less than ¼d. in the pound on the present rental. In 1905 there were 659 parishes
where the assessment was at the rate of a
penny in the pound, or less than a penny in
the pound.

The assessment of the tax upon personal
property never seems to have been carried
out beyond the first assessment. The explanation offered is, that the tax was regarded as a fixed charge upon the persons
upon whom it was first levied, and as these
persons ceased, through inability or death,
to be chargeable, the personal tax gradually
disappeared.

The idea behind the perpetuation of the
Land Tax was probably that the tax was a
rent to the Crown for the use of the land, as
the proprietorship of the land by the Crown
was then more clearly understood than it is
to-day.

The increment in land-values since 1692 has made the amount of the present yield from the Land Tax a grotesque absurdity. The present Land Tax ought to be repealed and some scheme applied which will secure for the community the social increment in land-values. Of this, more by-and-by.

The Inhabited House Duty

A sum of nearly £2,000,000 a year is raised by Inhabited House Duty. This tax is levied according to the following scale :—

	Where the Annual Value		
	Amounts to £20 but not above £40.	Exceeds £40 but not £60.	Exceeds £60.
Houses used solely as private dwellings	In the £. 3d.	In the £. 6d.	In the £. 9d.
Residential Shops, Hotels, Farmhouses, Lodging-houses . .	2d.	4d.	6d.

It is doubtful if this tax is worth the trouble of levying, and it is not always fair in its incidence, especially in the cases of the houses falling below £40, and residential shops, lodging-houses, and farmhouses. The enormous increase in rents within this generation has brought houses inhabited by working people within the taxable limit, and this makes a very undesirable addition to the rent of a house, a rent already far beyond that which a working man's income ought to have to bear. This tax has the pernicious effect of the old window-tax. It is a tax on healthy conditions, and tends to lower the standard of housing accommodation.

The rent of a house is not always a sure indication of the tenant's ability to pay taxes. The desired contribution to the revenue from people who ought to pay could be obtained as surely, say, by an addition to the Income Tax, as it is now got by the Inhabited House Duty, without any of the hardships which that tax frequently inflicts.

The two chief sources of revenue from Direct Taxation are the Estates Duties and the Income Tax. The rates of Estate Duties were fixed by Sir William Harcourt's Finance Act of 1894, and are as follows :—

Scale of .Estate Duties

Upon the principal value ascertained as provided by law, of all property, real or personal, settled or not settled, passing by deaths occurring after 1st August 1894, Estate Duty is leviable at the undermentioned rates :—

Where the Principal Value of the Estate		Rate of Duty per Cent.
Exceeds	And does not Exceed	
£	£	
100	500	1
500	1,000	2
1,000	10,000	3
10,000	25,000	4
25,000	50,000	$4\frac{1}{2}$
50,000	75,000	5
75,000	100,000	$5\frac{1}{2}$
100,000	150,000	6
150,000	250,000	$6\frac{1}{2}$
250,000	500,000	7
500,000	1,000,000	$7\frac{1}{2}$
1,000,000	...	8

An extra duty of 1 per cent. on settled estates.

Sir William Harcourt's reform of the Death Duties was the most drastic change in our taxation made in modern times. It is to be deplored that no positive national advantage has come from this reform. The increase of revenue obtained by the revision has been about eight millions a year, but since the scheme came into operation the annual amount spent upon the Army and the Navy has risen by £37,000,000 a year.

The only criticism I venture to offer here on Sir W. Harcourt's revision is, that it was unduly merciful to the large estates, and began the taxation of estates at a figure somewhat too low.

The Income Tax is the most important source of revenue. Last year it contributed £31,350,000 to the Exchequer. The return from the Income Tax has nearly doubled during the past ten years. It has been a more valuable contributor to the Exchequer than the revised Death Duties. In 1894 (the last complete year of the old Death Duties) the net receipts from Death Duties was £9,979,691. In 1906 the sum was £17,488,136. In 1894 the Income Tax contributed £15,649,000, and in 1906 a sum of £31,200,000. In 1904 the rate was 8d. in the pound; in 1906 the rate was 1s. in the pound.

In view of the importance which is attached to the possibility of Income Tax reform, a somewhat detailed statement of the system at present in force is necessary.

Unlike the Death Duties, which since Sir William Harcourt's re-arrangement have remained fixed, the Income Tax is regarded as a reservoir from which to draw in time of exceptional national need. In 1895–6 the rate of tax was 8d. in the pound; by 1902 it had risen to 1s. 3d., and in 1903 it declined to 11d. These fluctuations scarcely conform to Adam Smith's condition, that the taxpayer ought to know the amount of tax he is to be called upon to pay. But the explanation of the variation of the rate of Income Tax, often from year to year, is that the tax is regarded as an emergency tax, to be increased or decreased as circumstances may demand or permit.

An Income Tax fairly levied may be made to conform as nearly as possible to the ideal of a just tax. But the way in which the Income Tax is levied at present is unfair in its incidence. It presses with undue hardship upon certain classes, and permits others to escape with undeserved mercy.

CHAPTER VI

INCOME TAX REFORMS

To help to a clearer understanding of what may follow, it might be helpful to set out the particulars in regard to the present Income Tax abatements and rates.

INCOME TAX, 1905–6

One shilling in the pound on incomes exceeding £160 a year, abatements being allowed as follows :—

£160 on incomes exceeding £160 but not exceeding £400

150	,,	,,	400	,,	,,	500
120	,,	,,	500	,,	,,	600
70	,,	,,	600	,,	,,	700

No distinction whatever is made between the various sources of the income. The precarious income of the hard-working business man is taxed at the same rate as an equal income obtained from the rents of inherited property, or from the dividends of stocks or commercial investments. The professional or salaried man, whose income ceases with his own ability to work, is taxed equally with the person who need "take no thought for the morrow." The injustice of this is apparent.

Beyond the slight relief given to incomes between £160 and £700, the present system makes no attempt to graduate the tax in proportion to the ability of the individual. The tax takes £40 a year from an uncertain income of £800. It takes £500 from an unearned income of £10,000. There is no equality of sacrifice, no equality of payment for benefit received between two such contributions to the State. A tax of £40 on an income of £800 is a deduction which can be felt, but to take £500 from an income of £10,000 makes no appreciable difference to the income; it deprives the individual of no possible comfort; it simply reduces the individual's power by that amount to indulge in a luxury which is demoralising to everybody it touches.

The Income Tax as at present levied shows too little consideration for the smaller incomes, which are the largest in number, and too much regard for property. In 1853 Mr. Gladstone said: "I do not contest the opinion commonly entertained that intelligence and skill are too hardly pressed upon as compared with property." But in the years which have passed since those words were spoken, nothing has been done to lessen the evil.

These are objections which have always been felt and expressed in regard to the modern Income Tax. During the last sixty years innumerable Committees have sat to inquire into the mode of assessing and collecting the Income and Property Tax, and whether any mode of levying the same so as to render the tax more equitable could be adopted. All these Committees have taken much evidence, and debated the subject at great length. Many of them have presented elaborate reports, and made more or less valuable recommendations; but Chancellors of the Exchequer have ignored the reports, and have let matters rest until the discontent became strong once more, when it was again pacified by the appointment of another Committee.

During the Parliamentary Session of 1906 such a Select Committee, appointed by Mr. Asquith, presided over by Sir Charles Dilke, has sat, taken evidence, and reported.

The reference to this Committee was restricted. The Committee was prevented, by the terms of its appointment, from going beyond the questions of the practicability of graduating the Income Tax, and of differentiating, for the purpose of the tax, between "permanent" and "precarious" incomes. "It was beyond the scope of the inquiry to consider the desirability or equity, on general grounds of public policy, of the various proposals which were placed before the Committee."

The constitution of the Committee was such as to discourage any sanguine expectations that revolutionary changes would be recommended. They report, however, in favour of both graduation and differentiation, and recommend "that a compulsory personal declaration from each individual of total net income on which tax is payable is expedient, and would do much to prevent the evasion and avoidance of Income Tax which at present prevail."

These recommendations are all valuable, and especially is it gratifying to have the explicit statement of the importance of a personal declaration of total income from each individual. At present a person is required, in the personal declaration, to give only such income as has not already been taxed at source, unless he desires to claim some abatement, when it is necessary for him to prove that his total income is within the limit to entitle him to the abatement he claims. But in all cases where a person's income is above the abatement limit of £700 the Revenue Authorities do not require a full statement of income, but only of such portions as have not been taxed at the source. The dividends from investments are paid, less the Income Tax, the Income Tax being always collected where it is made, that is, at "the source." This system of collection at source has many advantages, chief amongst which are:—

It has been found to work well in practice.

It secures, under circumstances where evasion is difficult, two-thirds of the present Income Tax.

It secures Income Tax upon the dividends of foreign holders of shares in British Companies.

It secures economy in the cost of collection. The only serious drawback to the system of collecting the Income Tax at source has been that no reliable information could be furnished by the assessment returns of the number of individuals with total incomes of specified amounts. The absence of authentic statistical information as to the number of rich people, and the amounts of their respective incomes, is a disgrace to the Revenue Authorities, and is a serious hindrance to arriving at necessary facts bearing on wealth distribution. If the recommendation of the Committee, that each individual should be required to give a return of his total net income, whether already taxed or not, were carried out, we should then have the material for putting every individual into his proper compartment, and the way to graduating and differentiating the amount of the tax would be open.

Taxation reform, let me repeat, must follow on the line of abolishing Indirect Taxation, of transferring the taxes to incomes and estates, and of the increasingly heavy taxation of large incomes and big fortunes. The report of Sir Charles Dilke's Committee concedes everything the Socialist could wish as to the practicability of carrying out the Socialist plan of taxation. The principle and the practicability admitted, the rest becomes a question of detail and degree.

CHAPTER VII

THE DISTRIBUTION OF WEALTH

WE now digress somewhat to consider to what extent the wealth of the country is available for increased taxation. It will be remembered that in the earlier chapter we declared the Socialist object to be to secure social wealth for social use. Modern industry tends more and more to give large incomes to individuals without any labour or effort on the part of the receivers, such incomes being drawn from capital invested in companies, and in the work or management of which the shareholder takes no part. The abortive Select Committee which sat in 1861 printed a rejected report by its Chairman in which these words appear: " In one sense, *all* incomes are dependent upon labour; neither rents, interest of money, dividends of companies, nor dividends in the funds, can accrue without the labour of those who till the land, employ the money, work the company, or, out of their industry, provide the revenue to pay the public dividends; but 'spontaneous' incomes are distinguishable by this—the labour of the owners of such incomes is not requisite for their production. They are free to employ their talents, their labour or their time, in any way they please; the income derived from the investment of their capital needs not their assistance."

Since 1861 there has been a then undreamt-of development of incomes to which this description applies.   Let the Returns to the Board of Inland Revenue tell the tale.

Total Gross Amount of Income brought under Review for the Period 1885 to 1905

Year.	Total Gross Amounts.
1885	£631,467,132
1890	669,358,613
1895–6	677,769,850
1896–7	704,741,608
1897–8	734,461,246
1898–9	762,667,309
1899–1900. . .	791,735,413
1900–1	833,355,513
1901–2	866,993,453
1902–3	879,638,546
1903–4	902,758,585
1904–5	912,129,680
1905–6 Not yet available.	

Particulars of the way in which the gross assessment of £912,129,680 for 1904–5 is made up are important to an understanding of the possibilities of Income Tax revision.

TABLE SHOWING IN DETAIL FOR THE UNITED KINGDOM THE GROSS INCOME BROUGHT UNDER THE REVIEW OF THE INLAND REVENUE DEPARTMENT FOR THE YEAR 1904-5:—

Class 1 (Schedule A). Profits from the ownership of—

Lands	£52,257,999	
Houses	201,572,703	
Other property	1,296,701	
		£255,127,403

Class 2 (Schedule B). Profits from the occupation of lands (Farmers' profits mainly) 17,479,547

Class 3 (Schedule C). Profits from British, Indian, Colonial, and Foreign *Government* securities 45,580,640

Class 4 (Schedule D). Profits from Businesses, Concerns, Professions, Employments (except those of a public nature. See Class 5), and certain interest—

I. Businesses, Professions, &c. (including salaries of employés), other than those enumerated below . .	£365,763,420	
II. Railways in the United Kingdom	41,211,420	
III. Mines	21,235,729	
IV. Gasworks	7,606,530	

V.	Ironworks	3,134,867
VI.	Waterworks	5,327,082
VII.	Canals, &c.	3,608,443
VIII.	Quarries	1,729,091
IX.	Markets, Tolls, &c.	853,993
X.	Fishings in the United Kingdom and Sporting	
	Rights in Ireland	222,095
XI.	Cemeteries	181,620
XII.	Salt Springs or Works and Alum Works .	153,737
XIII.	Indian, Colonial, and Foreign Securities .	11,404,180
XIV.	Coupons	10,465,377
XV.	Railways out of the United Kingdom	14,551,530
XVI.	Loans secured on the Public Rates .	9,040,063
XVII.	Other Interest	4,333,739
XVIII.	Other Profits	3,732,561
XIX.	Profits from the Occupation of Lands .	12,322
		———————
		£504,567,799
Class 5 (Schedule E). Salaries of Government, Corporation, and Public		
	Company Officials	89,374,291
		———————
Total Gross Income brought under the Review of the Department, 1904–5 .		£912,129,680
		———————

In the ten years from 1885 to 1895 the
Gross Assessments to Income Tax increased
by £46,300,000 only. In the second decade,
from 1895 to 1905, there was an unbroken
record of large annual increases amounting
in the aggregate to £235,000,000 a year.
Comparing the gross amount of income
arising from the ownership of lands, houses,
&c., for the year 1904–5 with that for 1895–6,
there was a net increase of £44,511,000, or
21.1 per cent. There was a decrease in land
of £3,150,000, or 5.6 per cent.; and an increase as regards houses of £47,032,000, or
30.4 per cent.

Businesses, Concerns, Professions, &c.,
show an increase of £147,948,000, or 41.1
per cent. during the ten years; and salaries of
Government, Corporation, and Public Company Officials increased during the period
from £53,037,000 to £89,374,000, or 67.6
per cent. The conversion of private concerns
into Public Companies has had the effect of
increasing the amount assessed under the
last-named head at the expense of the class
"Profits from Businesses and Concerns."

The outstanding feature of the comparison of the Gross Income of 1881 with 1905
is the enormous increase in the profits of

"Public Companies." In 1881 the gross profits of "Public Companies," including railways, mines, canals, gasworks, waterworks, and commercial companies, were £76,000,000. In 1905 this item had risen to £247,332,310, or over 200 per cent. This is all "spontaneous" income, income which accrues to the recipients independently of their own labours.

The total income of the nation is estimated (1904) at £1,710,000,000. In 1884 it was put by Sir Louis Mallet at £1,289,000,000. The increase in the nation's annual income in these twenty-one years is £421,000,000, and the profits, &c., returned for Income Tax account for £280,000,000 of the increase, the profits assessed under Schedule D (from Businesses, Companies, &c.) accounting for no less than £212,000,000 of this increase.

The next point to be considered is the number of individuals by whom the sum of £912,129,680 (the gross amount of income brought under the review of the Revenue department in 1905) is received. Though there are no absolutely unimpeachable statistics to explain this question, there is a sufficient agreement amongst investigators to arrive at a fairly trustworthy estimate.

Sir Henry Primrose, the Chairman of the Board of Inland Revenue, in his evidence before the Select Committee on Income Tax, states that it would be a reasonable conclusion to fix the number of individuals with incomes between £160 and £700 at 800,000, and the number with incomes above £700 at 300,000 ; that is, the total number of individuals with incomes over £160 a year may be set down at 1,100,000. This may be taken as a fairly liberal estimate.

Mr. Chiozza Money, M.P., to whose painstaking investigations into the distribution of the national income all interested in the subject are much indebted, put in as evidence before the Select Committee the following analysis of the distribution of the nation's income. His figures were accepted with but slight modification by the official witnesses from Somerset House.

It is not necessary to trouble our readers with a detailed statement as to the way in which this analysis of the distribution of the National Income has been worked out. Those interested further will find full information in the Evidence of Sir Charles Dilke's Committee.

INCOME OF THE UNITED KINGDOM IN 1904

Distribution as between (1) those with £700 per annum and upwards, (2) those with £160 to £700 per annum, (3) those with less than £160 per annum.

	Number.	Income.
A. Persons with incomes of £700 per annum and upwards and their families (275,000 × 5)	1,375,000	£585,000,000
B. Persons with incomes between £160 and £700 and families (750,000 × 5) .	3,750,000	245,000,000
C. Persons with less than £160 and their families	37,875,000	880,000,000
	43,000,000	£1,710,000,000

The Chairman of the Board of Inland Revenue has made an analysis of the distribution of incomes above £5000 into grades, and has submitted the following very conservative estimate :—

ESTIMATE OF NUMBER OF PERSONS WITH INCOMES OVER £5000 A YEAR

Class.	Number.	Total Income.
Over £40,000 a year	250	£20,000,000
Between £20,000 and £40,000	750	21,000,000
,, 10,000 ,, 20,000	2,500	35,000,000
,, 5,000 ,, 10,000	6,500	45,000,000
Total over £5000 a year . .	10,000	121,000,000

This estimate, which appears to be founded largely on imagination, and a desire to minimise the amount of the national income appropriated by a few persons, is not endorsed by any impartial authority.

The following estimate is made by averaging the conclusions of a number of witnessess who gave evidence on the point before Sir Charles Dilke's Committee, and may, I think, be accepted as being as nearly correct as the meagre data available will enable a correct conclusion to be formed.

ANOTHER ESTIMATE OF THE NUMBER OF PERSONS WITH INCOMES OVER £5000

		Persons.	
Between £5,000 and £6,000	.	6000	. £38,000,000
„ 6,000 „ 10,000	.	5000	. 40,000,000
„ 10,000 „ 20,000	.	3500	. 45,000,000
„ 20,000 „ 40,000	.	1100	. 30,000,000
Over 40,000		400	. 30,000,000

Aggregate income of 16,000 persons, £183,000,000
Add for evasion 17,000,000

Total . . . £200,000,000

Deducting this sum from the total of £585,000,000 income of all over £700 a year, we get £402,000,000 as the total income of 259,000 persons with incomes between £700 and £5000 a year.

The Death Duties Returns tell the same tale of enormous wealth concentrated in a

few hands.   In the last eleven years (1895–
1905) the wills of 78 millionaires have been
proved.   It may be interesting and instruc-
tive to set out the particulars for each year.

Year.	Number of Estates over £1,000,000.	Total Value.
1895	8	£8,725,000
1896	5	5,441,000
1897	7	14,735,614
1898	9	11,654,846
1899	12	28,172,899
1900	9	13,603,453
1901	8	38,529,868
1902	4	11,981,785
1903	7	14,605,488
1904	1	5,941,926
1905	8	13,547,617
	78	£166,939,496

In the last eleven years seventy-eight
people have died possessed of £167,000,000!
These estates have contributed to the State
in Death Duties a total sum of £13,360,000,
leaving £153,640,000 to be transferred to
other private individuals that they might
continue to exploit the community with it.

The total value of 194 estates ranging
between £500,000 and a million left in the
same period aggregates to £150,000,000.

With all the foregoing facts at our dis-
posal we are now in a position to begin to
outline our scheme of taxation reform.

CHAPTER VIII

FISCAL AND OTHER REFORMS

THE State has no right to tax individuals unless it is prepared to put the money thus obtained to a more useful purpose than that to which it was formerly devoted.

The just and beneficial needs of the community must be the measure of taxation. Public requirements, social reform, ought not to remain unsatisfied so long as there is untaxed rent, interest, and profit appropriated by individuals.

The amount of revenue it is desired to raise at any time will be determined by the cost of carrying out needed and agreed-upon social reforms.

Local and national reforms wait for money. In the sphere of Local Government, the health, the education, the comfort of the people are being sacrificed for the want of means. The burden of local rates is felt to be so oppressive that only expenditure which cannot be obviated is incurred. Between 1880 and 1903 the local rates in England and Wales have increased per head of the population from 17s. 6d. to £1, 10s. 1d. The Total Rates raised by local bodies in Great Britain in 1903–4 amounted to £58,256,864, being an increase in fifteen years of £27,256,157, or 87 per cent.

It is important to take note of the fact that the increase of municipal rates is accounted for by the larger expenditure upon Education, the Poor, and Public Health. In 1905 there were 1,342,892 more children on the registers of the Elementary Schools in Great Britain than in 1891, and in 1903 the sum taken from the rates for aiding the schools was £16,273,877, while in 1891 the amount was £7,649,566. There has been an increase in the annual sum spent in Relief of the Poor in the last fifteen years of over £5,000,000.

Many of the public services formerly local in their character have now assumed a national character. The education of the children, the provision of work for the workless, the treatment of the aged poor and infirm, are increasingly recognised as being national, and not merely local, obligations. In recognition of these obligations the State collects nearly £30,000,000 a year of taxation (including the Education Grants), which it hands over to the Local Authorities to assist their work of local administration.

In this system of Grants-in-Aid we have a happy blending of the spheres of responsibilities of national government and local administration. The ideal administration is that which combines in the most exact proportions national contribution and national control with local contribution and local management. The proportions will vary in different matters. In Education and in Poor Law the cost of the systems should equitably be borne chiefly by the nation, demanding only such local contribution as will excuse some measure of local management and will stimulate local patriotism to the highest efficiency.

The question of national taxation cannot in these days be considered apart from the kindred subject of Local Government, and to an ever-increasing extent will the hitherto distinct spheres of the two authorities commingle. For most purposes of well-being

will the nation have to be considered as a
unit. With the object of establishing at least
a national minimum of well-being, if not a
more uniform condition, the poorer parts
of the country will not have to be left to
struggle as best they can with their insufficient means to educate their children, and
deal with the problems of unemployment,
of public health, and of old age. The whole
national resources will have to be available
to the whole nation for treating these
problems.

The Socialist Budget would provide for a
very considerable increase of the Grants-
in-Aid, retaining for the Central Government just sufficient control or inspection
over the expenditure as would not interfere
with the reasonable freedom of the Local
Authority. The Grant-in-Aid should be a
payment by results, the Local Authority
being encouraged to exert itself to the
utmost of its ability by the promise of a
reward in proportion to its success.

The removal of the greater part of the
Education Rate and the Poor Rate from the
Local Rates would liberate a considerable
capacity which might be utilised to some extent to carry out desired local improvements

of a more strictly local character, and which now are left undone because of the want of money.

The first Socialist Budget would, therefore, be called upon to provide for :—

> The Transfer of the Cost of Education to the State.
>
> Some provision for Dealing with the Unemployed.
>
> The Treatment of the Infirm and Aged.
>
> The Abolition of Indirect Taxation.
>
> The Establishment of a "Free Breakfast Table."
>
> The payment of Returning Officers' Expenses.
>
> Payment of Members.

The transfer of the cost of Education to the State would involve an obligation to provide, in round figures, say, £20,000,000 a year in addition to the sum which is given from the Imperial Exchequer at present. It is important not to forget that this would be a transfer and not an addition to the total taxation of the country.

The Unemployed problem is not to be solved by Grants-in-Aid from the National Exchequer. But by that means a great deal may be done to relieve temporary distress. Every district in the country has improvements it would like to carry out if it had the means. It is not to be expected, if the unemployed be set to work, that the work will be done as cheaply as by the employment of efficient and trained labour. But any extra cost will have been wisely incurred in preserving the manhood of the men employed, and in preventing them from sinking into the painful class of social derelicts. Every Local Authority ought to have some elastic organisation which can expand or contract so as to absorb the unemployed in useful work at any given time. The sum of £200,000 set aside in 1906 for distribution to the Local Authorities is a precedent a Socialist President of the Local Government Board will put before a Socialist Chancellor of the Exchequer, and his plea would certainly result in a sum of not less than £2,000,000 a year being set aside, if required, for a similar purpose.

The community, unlike the individual, never dies. The State can not only afford, but has a duty to look to the future. Certain schemes which would give ultimate benefit are not promoted because, whilst the cost will fall immediately, the return will be postponed. The State is just the body to undertake such schemes. Such a scheme is afforestation. Individual land-owners will not undertake the work because they themselves may not live to reap the benefits. The initial capital and cost of labour will have to be provided from State funds. Out of the money set apart for the Unemployed an extensive scheme of afforestation may be financed.

Afforestation is a proposal which should be urged on the merits of the importance and necessity of afforestation, and only incidentally as a scheme for relieving the unemployed. Our imports of timber and wood in various forms now amount to about £30,000,000 a year in value. There is no insuperable difficulty in the way of all our timber requirements being, in time, supplied from our own forests. Dr. Schlich, the great authority on Forestry, calculates that nine million acres would be required to produce the present value of forest imports. We have twelve million acres of land which are unsuitable for cultivation, but which are admirably fitted for tree-growing.

The planting of these acres would, of course, be gradual, and, if they were planted at the rate of 400,000 a year, at least 20,000 labourers—corresponding to a population of 100,000 people—would be employed. At the end of thirty years, when all the twelve million acres were planted, permanent employment would be given to about 200,000 labourers, representing a population of a million people.

In addition to the people directly employed in the forests, there would be a large population provided for in supplying the needs of the forest workers. Germany provides a useful illustration of the possibilities of forestry. There, 12 per cent. of the total population is employed in the forests, or in connection with the forests. There are one million persons directly employed in the woods, and three million persons in working the trees into timber and into forms for manufacturing use.

Much of the land which would be utilised for afforestation would be land which is, at present, waste. Its value is negligible. The whole of the twelve million acres could probably be bought for as many pounds. That would not involve an annual charge for interest and repayment of more than £600,000. But as the acquirement of the land would be gradual, only some portion of that charge would have to be met. The cost of planting, draining, and fencing is set down by experts at from £4 to £5 per acre.

Regard for our national welfare in the future, consideration for utilising the land for its natural purpose, the desire to do something for the unemployed—all should respond to the claims which afforestation has for doing much to fulfil these needs.

CHAPTER IX

OLD AGE PENSIONS

ON the 14th March 1906 the following motion was passed by the House of Commons without a division: "That in the opinion of this House a measure is urgently needed in order that, out of funds provided by taxation, provision can be made for the payment of a pension to all the aged subjects of His Majesty in the United Kingdom."

In speaking to this motion Mr. Asquith said: "On the broad grounds of principle on which this motion has been put forward, not only is there no reluctance on the part of the Government to accept it, but there is the strongest and keenest possible desire, by every means we can find available and practicable, to further the object the motion has in view. This is one of the subjects, few and rare, I am sorry to say, as to which I believe there is no difference of opinion in any part of the House." The Chancellor then went on to point out that the prospect of carrying out such a proposal was more remote than it was ten years ago, "our annual expenditure having, in these ten years, risen by £40,000,000." The only hope of realising an Old Age Pension scheme lay in retrenchment in Army and Navy expenditure.

This reply was not very encouraging. To a deputation which waited upon the Prime Minister and Mr. Asquith in November of the same year, the Chancellor was somewhat more definite, but not more committal. Perhaps the certainty of a very large surplus next April had lightened up the honourable gentleman's horizon.

The cost of a scheme of Old Age Pensions can only be estimated approximately. It is impossible to estimate to what extent people not in fairly comfortable circumstances would take advantage of a universal scheme.

A Departmental Committee was appointed in 1900 to arrive at some estimate of the cost of such a scheme as that recommended by the Select Committee which reported in 1899. The scheme of this Committee was not universal. It ruled out all who, within twenty years, had been committed to penal servitude or to imprisonment without the option of a fine, who had received poor-law relief within twenty years, who had an income of more than ten shillings a week, and who could not produce evidence of having practised thrift.

The cost of such a scheme in 1901 was estimated to be as follows :—

COST OF OLD AGE PENSION SCHEME

	United Kingdom.
Estimated number of persons of over sixty-five years in 1901 . .	2,016,000
Deduct :—	
1. For those with 10s. a week of income	741,000
2. For Paupers	515,000
3. For Criminals and Lunatics .	32,000
4. For the Thriftless . . .	72,700
Total Deductions . . .	1,360,700
Estimated number of Pensioners	655,300
Estimated Cost	£9,976,000
Add for Administration . . .	299,000
Total Estimated Cost . . .	£10,275,000
In round figures	£10,300,000

That was the estimated cost of a pension of from 5s. to 7s. a week (ranging according to the cost of living in the locality) at the age of sixty-five. The following further estimates were made for schemes to begin with a pensionable age at seventy and seventy-five :—

1901.	65.	70.	75.
1901	£10,300,000	£5,950,000	£2,950,000
1911	12,650,000	7,450,000	3,700,000
1921	15,650,000	9,550,000	4,950,000

It is certain that no Parliament, least of all a Socialist Parliament, would agree to establish a scheme with the exemptions suggested by the Select Committee. The scheme must be universal, and the cost would, therefore, be higher than the Committee's estimate. It would not be wise to make any considerable reduction for pensions not claimed, so, to be on the safe side, £20,000,000 may be set down as the initial cost of an Old Age Pension scheme.

But as a set-off against this a considerable saving of Poor Law Relief would be effected. How much, it is difficult to say. The last returns of Local Taxation which deal with 1904–5 give the following sums as having been spent in the year on " Relief of the Poor and matters connected therewith :"—

England and Wales .	£13,851,981
Scotland. . . .	1,402,354
Ireland	1,253,355
Total of Poor Law Relief	£16,507,690

This sum includes, of course, a large amount which would necessarily be expended if Old Age Pensions were established. A humanised Poor Law would still require to maintain institutions in which the infirm and aged without relatives might find an honourable and a comfortable home. The saving in Poor Law Relief by Old Age Pensions might be anything from five to ten million pounds a year. There would be a corresponding relief to local taxation, or, preferably, a transfer of the amount saved to payment for the improvement of other local services.

Payment of Members

The present Parliament has unanimously declared in favour of Returning Officers' charges being a public charge, and by an overwhelming majority once more approved the principle of Payment of Members. We are assured by the Government that nothing but the difficulty of finding the money stands in the way of these reforms being carried out. To pay 670 members £300 a year each would require £261,000, and the average annual cost of providing for Returning Officers' charges might be put at the liberal figure of £139,000 a year. To carry out this Liberal promise would therefore require £400,000 a year.

ABOLITION OF INDIRECT TAXATION

For eighty years a Free Breakfast-table has been a shibboleth of Radicalism. The foregoing chapters, dealing with Indirect Taxation, show how far from realisation is this oft-preached reform. To establish a Free Breakfast-table the duties require to be removed from cocoa, coffee, chicory, dried fruits, sugar, and tea. To do this would involve a loss of revenue amounting to £14,000,000. We do not propose, for reasons to be stated later, to interfere in the first Socialist Budget with the taxes upon Spirits, Beer, and Wines, nor upon Tobacco.

Further remissions of taxation would be made by removing all Licence duties upon trade, except in the case of Drink licences and Tobacco. It is important that traders who deal in excisable articles should be licensed as a protection to the revenue. For this reason, and for the same reason that the Drink taxes are to be maintained, it is not proposed to interfere with licences for the sale and manufacture of spirits and beer.

The revenue from Excise Licences of all descriptions amounts to £4,365,000. The

Licences to carry on the Drink and Tobacco trades raise £2,250,000 a year. Other licences which might be described as taxes on luxury which the Socialist Budget would not repeal are those upon male servants, private carriages, motors, armorial bearings, and guns.

The licence duties which the Socialist Budget would abolish would be those upon chemists, auctioneers, house-agents, hawkers, plate-dealers, pawnbrokers, refreshment houses, and hackney carriages. The loss of revenue by the abolition of these licences would amount to about £270,000 only.

There remain two other objectionable heads of revenue which would find no place in a Socialist National Balance Sheet—the profit from the Post Office and the Stamp Duties. Improvements in the wages and conditions of labour in the lower grades of the Postal Service would absorb a considerable part of the present annual profit of £5,000,000, and the rest might, with benefit, be utilised for cheapening the cost to the public of postal rates and services. The withdrawal of the Post Office surplus from relieving the rich of taxation, and the abolition of the Stamp Duties would involve a sacrifice of revenue to the extent of £13,000,000 a year.

The abolition of Indirect Taxation, &c.,
to the extent outlined would cause a reduction of the present revenue by the sum of
£27,420,000, made up as follows :—

Free Breakfast-table . .	£13,341,000
Licence Duties abolished .	270,000
Post Office subsidy . .	5,000,000
Stamp Duties . . .	8,150,000
Inhabited House Duty .	1,950,000
Land Tax	720,000
Taxation Remitted .	£29,431,000

We may now summarise the proposed
additions and remissions of taxation, and see
what amount of new taxation will require
to be imposed to carry out this programme.

REFORMS SUGGESTED

(To be met from the Imperial Revenue)

For Education	£20,000,000
For Unemployed and Afforestation	2,000,000
For Old Age Pensions . . .	20,000,000
For Payment of Members and Re-turning Officers' Fees . .	400,000
Total	£42,400,000
Taxation Remitted . .	29,431,000
Total of Deficit . .	£71,831,000

The question now is, how to raise seventy-
two millions of revenue. But it must not
be forgotten that fifty-two millions of this
is not additional taxation.

CHAPTER X

IT is to the Income Tax, the Death Duties, and to Land Values we turn to make up the seventy-two millions of revenue we need.

THE INCOME TAX

In the previous chapter on the Income Tax we have indicated the principles upon which it should be based. In the analysis of the distribution of the national income we have shown the enormous, unexhausted, taxable capacity of that one-thirtieth of the population who take one-third of the national income. The three things to aim at in the levying of the Income Tax are (1) graduation of tax according to size of income, (2) differentiation according to the nature of the income, (3) to derive the revenue from large and unearned incomes mainly.

It is important that any new system of

Income Tax assessment should conform to five conditions :—

1. It should, as far as is consistent with securing the new objects aimed at, not be a violent and radical change from the present system.

2. It should aim at simplicity, even if the attainment of simplicity involves some little loss of revenue. The method of assessing and raising the tax should be of a character to be easily understood. Simplicity of taxation is generally consistent with economy of collection.

3. It should be in conformity with popular ideas of just taxation, so as to secure the maximum of co-operation from the tax-payers.

4. It should be levied in such a way as to afford little opportunity of evasion.

5. It should be capable of automatic increase of poundage, that is to say, it should be possible to increase the amount of the tax without in any way changing the system of levying and collecting.

The three objects to be attained, namely, graduation, differentiation, and the diversion of excessive incomes to social use, can be secured without violence to any of the five conditions enumerated.

The relief given by the abolition of Indirect Taxation would remove the need for
any remission of Income Tax on incomes
between £160 and £700 a year, which, with
a slight simplification of abatements, might
remain as at present, with the tax at 1s.
in the pound. It may be worth while to
point out that incomes up to £700 a year
do not pay 1s. in the pound tax. Allowing
for the abatements, the rate runs at from 1¼d.
in the pound on incomes of £180, to 10¾d.
in the pound on those of £700. This re-
minder is necessary to those with incomes
subject to abatement who complain of the
burden of a shilling Income Tax.

A perfectly just and equitable system of
levying, graduating, and differentiating the
Income Tax cannot be evolved by one effort
out of the chaos of the present official knowledge. The most one might hope to accomplish in the first Budget would be to lay the
foundation of a better system, and afterwards
to build in the light of experience and more
accurate knowledge.

I would suggest, therefore, that a beginning should be made by the special taxation
of incomes over £5000 a year. The reasons
for limiting the application of graduation and

differentiation to such incomes for a start are :—

1. That by limiting the operation of the changes to a small number of persons (estimated at 16,000) the difficulties incidental to any change will be reduced to a minimum.

2. That the special treatment of incomes over £5000 would be immeasurably popular (except, of course, with the possessors of these incomes).

3. This limitation would restrict the opposition to a very small number of individuals.

4. It would not be difficult to discover, with approximate completeness, all who were liable to this special treatment.

5. It would be very valuable as an experiment, and the machinery having been established would only require increasing to deal with any extension which might, as the result of experience, be considered desirable, either in the way of carrying the system down to incomes below £5000, or in increasing the super-tax.

6. To carry this out would require little addition to the present staff of the Revenue Department.

7. The additional revenue would be very considerable.

8. Both graduation and differentiation could be easily applied.

The possibilities of evasion of the super-tax on such incomes are very small. The probability of detection is great. This is so, because the sources of large incomes are either obvious or easily traced, being either for real property, or dividends in public companies, or salaries which are stated in Reports and Balance Sheets. The returns in the cases of wealthy people living on un-earned incomes are usually made by agents and solicitors, who keep precise accounts, are reputable, and have little interest in evasion.

The only classes of income where evasion to any great extent would be possible are some of those assessed under Schedule D. But the possibility of evasion to any great extent gets more remote, owing to the tendency for profits to come more in the form of company dividends. Out of £502,402,516 assessed under Schedule D, about four-fifths is assessed at source.

The first year would demand considerable effort in ascertaining who were liable to the super-tax, but the work once done would be done, to a great extent, for many years.

In doing this work material would have been obtained of future use for (1) extending the operation of the super-tax to incomes below £5000 a year, (2) sociological purposes bearing on the distribution of wealth and tendency of wealth distribution.

On page 54 I give a Table of the number of persons with incomes over £5000 a year. We require to raise £30,000,000 by the proposed super-tax on these incomes. This would involve the following rates of super-tax on different grades of income:—

Income.	Aggregate Amount.	Rate of Super-tax in £.	Revenue.
Between—	£		£
£5,000 and £6,000	38,000,000	1s.	1,900,000
6,000 ,, 10,000	40,000,000	2s.	4,000,000
10,000 ,, 20,000	45,000,000	3s.	6,750,000
20,000 ,, 40,000	30,000,000	4s. 6d.	6,750,000
Over £40,000 .	30,000,000	6s.	9,000,000
			28,400,000
Ten per cent. on incomes at present evading tax			1,700,000
Total of Increased Revenue . .			30,100,000

To console the possessors of incomes in the higher grade, say, £50,000 a year, to the payment of an Income Tax of 7s. in the pound, we may remind them that they still retain £33,500 a year, which is a very generous payment by labour to them for the privilege of seeing them exist in gorgeous splendour and sumptuous idleness. Such a tax, too, is moderation itself compared to the Income Tax of 4s. in the pound imposed in 1692, in an age when the margin between the general incomes and the cost of necessaries was very small. It will console all with incomes below £20,000 a year to remember how much more generously the Socialist of the twentieth century treats him in his abundance than the Parliament of landowners treated themselves and their fellows in the seventeenth century. In 1799 Parliament imposed an Income Tax of 2s. in the pound on all incomes over £60 a year.

CHAPTER XI

THE DEATH DUTIES

WE must now turn to the Estate Duties and see to what extent it is possible for them to assist us in making up the forty million pounds still required.

Taking the figures given by the Board of Inland Revenue for the year 1905–6 we find that the Capital Values of 3924 estates exceeding £10,000 amounted in the aggregate to £195,740,000. These 3924 estates contributed duty varying from 4 per cent. to 8 per cent., amounting altogether to £11,443,032. There were 76,443 estates valued below £10,000, the aggregate value of these being £76,433,000. Upon these the duty was £2,142,751. As these facts have a distinct bearing on the incidence of the duties, it might be well to put them in the form of a table.

PARTICULARS OF ESTATES PAYING ESTATE DUTY, 1905

Capital Value.	Number.	Aggregate Value.	Duty Paid.
£		£	£
Not exceeding 10,000	76,443	76,433,000	2,142,757
Exceeding . 10,000	3,924	195,740,000	11,443,032

The changes in the rates of duty we propose are as follows:—

Class.		Present Rate per Cent.	Suggested Rate per Cent.
Between—			
£100 and	£500	1	1
500 ,,	1,000	2	2
1,000 ,,	10,000	3	3
10,000 ,,	25,000	4	6
25,000 ,,	50,000	4½	7½
50,000 ,,	75,000	5	10
75,000 ,,	100.000	5½	12½
100,000 ,,	150,000	6	15
150,000 ,,	250,000	6½	17½
250,000 ,,	500,000	7	20
500,000 ,,	1,000,000	7½	25
Over 1,000,000	. .	8	50

Calculating the duty at these new rates on the respective Capital Values of 1905–6, the revenue would amount to nearly £30,000,000, or an increase of £17,000,000.

The moral and economic justification for the suggested taxation of large fortunes at the rates mentioned will be found in the first chapter of this book. To what has been said there it is only necessary to add that these duties are not the taxation of those persons who have earned or possessed these estates. These individuals are dead and gone. They have enjoyed their fortunes so long as they could use them. These duties, at the most,

F

simply reduce the good luck of other individuals who come into the possession of great wealth to the production of which they have contributed nothing.

TAXATION OF LAND VALUES

We have no exact knowledge of the amount of the Site Values of this country. Estimates differ widely according to the purpose the estimate is destined to serve. Taking the mean between the extreme estimates, we may set down the annual value of the land of the country at £250,000,000. This capitalised gives a sum of £6,000,000,000. A tax of a penny in the pound on the capital value would bring in a revenue of £25,000,000 a year.

The balance of advantage is in favour of making the Land Values Tax a national one. Exceptional land values are not created wholly by local effort or by local causes. Liverpool, London, Glasgow, owe their existence and their prosperity to their respective situations, which are natural advantages, and which ought not in justice to be enjoyed solely by those who live upon the sites. Every town and village in the country contributes to the prosperity of every other part. The nation is a unit ; its resources and its obligations should be mutually shared.

A national Land Tax does not forbid site values being made the basis of local taxation also. Indeed, after the Imperial Tax of a penny in the pound has been imposed, there remains abundant scope for the local authority to put in a just claim for a further contribution to local expenditure from site values. In New Zealand, Land Values are taxed both for State and local revenue.

Land Values are so obviously not created by individual effort, that the justice of taking the increment for the use of the community appeals to those who may have some difficulty in grasping the working of the " Unearned Increment " in commercial concerns, where, however, it operates just as truly though not so obviously.

The imposition of an Imperial Tax of one penny in the pound on the capital value of the site would be a beginning but by no means the end of the process of diverting socially created rent of land into the public exchequer. Taxation will do something towards that end ; but taxation would be a long, irritating, and untrustworthy way of

trying to secure the whole annual value of
the land for the community.   The taxation of
Land Values is not a land reform.   The most
it could do would be to cut down monopoly
rents which now obtain through land being
kept out of the market; and as a means of
raising revenue it fulfils every condition of
just taxation.   But to get the full usefulness
and the full value of the land for the community, there is no way but for the State to
own the land.

THE LIQUOR TAXES

For several reasons we propose to retain
the taxes upon alcoholic drinks.   To abolish
them would be to give the amount of the
taxes as an annual gift to the "Trade,"
which is, at present, one of the wealthiest
and most profitable.   The Drink Trade, first
by the monopoly of licence, and secondly,
by the operation of economic forces which
are making all trades tend towards monopoly, has become a gigantic monopoly.   If
the taxes were abolished the practical absence
of competition in the trade would enable the
brewers and licence-holders to retain their
present prices, thus adding to their profits,

as already stated, the amount of the taxes now levied on their commodities. The retention of the taxes and licences may be rightly regarded as payment by "The Trade" to the State for the monopoly it enjoys as the gift of the State.

If the taxation of liquor does in any degree restrict the consumption, that is another reason for the retention of the duties. The Drink Traffic is one which the State would be justified in taxing for the sole purpose of discouraging the use of alcoholic drinks. The taxation of the Drink Trade ought to be retained, too, in view of the drastic reorganisation or control of the traffic which a Socialist Parliament would make one of its first pieces of work. In such a scheme the whole question of the taxation of liquors would be considered in its general relation to the whole drink problem.

CHAPTER XII

THE SOCIALIST'S BUDGET

WE are now in a position to present our first Socialist Budget in proper arrangement.

THE SOCIALIST BUDGET

Taxes Repealed

Customs Duties—

Cocoa	£273,000
Coffee and Chicory . .	230,000
Dried Fruits	475,000
Sugar	6,178,000
Tea	6,185,000
Total Customs Duties	**£13,341,000**

Excise Duties—

Stamps	£8,150,000
Land Tax	720,000
House Duty . . .	1,950,000
Licences	270,000
Post Office subsidy . .	5,000,000
Total Excise Duties .	**£16,090,000**
Total of Taxes Repealed	**£29,431,000**

Additional Taxation Imposed

Income Tax (Increase) . . .	£30,100,000
Estate Duties (Increase) . . .	17,000,000
Land Values	25,000,000
Total New Taxation . . .	£72,100,000
Deduct Taxation Repealed .	29,431,000
Surplus	£42,669,000

Disposal of Surplus

Education (to replace Local Education rate abolished) . . .	£20,000,000
Old Age Pensions (partly to relieve Local Poor Rate) . . .	20,000,000
Unemployed and Afforestation .	2,000,000
Payment of Members and Returning Officers' charges . . .	400,000
Total	£42,400,000

This Budget would relieve the working classes of £11,000,000 now paid upon their food. It would give the much-needed relief from House Duty to the struggling class trying to maintain a house rented beyond their means. It would relieve business of the Stamp Tax on commercial transactions. It would provide for great improvements in the pay of Post Office servants, and would give the public better facilities. It would enable the unemployed to be put to useful work. It would bring sunshine and some comfort into the lives of a million and a half old folks.   Last, but not least, it would give twenty-five millions a year of relief to the local rates of the country, and thereby make it possible to carry out many much-needed local requirements now impossible through the burden of rates.

The Socialist object as stated in the first chapter is to secure all socially created wealth for society.   Such a Budget as we have outlined would be a new beginning towards that end.   The end would be achieved when, by the social ownership of the instruments of wealth-production, society owned and controlled the wealth produced.   That is the Socialist goal.   Meanwhile, taxation may be used to palliate some of the evils which, in degree, must always exist so long as land and capital are the monopoly of individuals.

Printed by BALLANTYNE, HANSON & Co.
Edinburgh & London